Agricultural
Protection
and Trade

Agricultural Protection and Trade

Proposals for an International Policy

J. H. RICHTER

FREDERICK A. PRAEGER, *Publisher*
New York · London

FREDERICK A. PRAEGER, PUBLISHER
64 UNIVERSITY PLACE, NEW YORK 3, N.Y., U.S.A.
77–79 CHARLOTTE STREET, LONDON W. 1, ENGLAND

Published in the United States of America in 1964
by Frederick A. Praeger, Inc., Publisher

Library of Congress Catalog Card Number: 64-16687

Printed in the United States of America

Acknowledgment

THE PROPOSALS for an international accommodation on agricultural support and trade advanced in this study reiterate and update suggestions made over the past few years. By courtesy of the publications concerned, I have, in some sections, drawn on articles that I published in 1961, 1962, and 1963, especially those in *Kyklos, The Commercial and Financial Chronicle, The Journal of Farm Economics,* and the *International Journal of Agrarian Affairs.* Specific references are given in the text.

J. H. R.

Preface

THE PROBLEM to which the present study is devoted is not merely a conflict between the agricultural and general economic interests of the United States and those of the member countries of the European Economic Community or Common Market. Rather it is a wider issue that may touch upon the future of international trade in general: the problem of how to reconcile national support for agriculture, inevitable in most countries that can afford it, with the need for maintaining agricultural trade—how to reconcile with each other reasonable aspirations of agricultural interests in both importing and exporting areas. The situation existing between the United States and the European Economic Community will, however, not only serve the purpose of exemplification; it will also be treated specifically, for it is imperative that we prepare for a realistic agreement between these two powerful trading partners; nothing could help better bring about a solution of the more general problem.

In approaching a task of this kind, we should seek to walk a path of reason and compromise. It is good to look to classical antiquity for philosophical and practical guidance in this respect. Of the great Greek scholar Gilbert Murray it has once been said that he himself was very Greek—because of his utter trust in reason and a capacity to put himself into the shoes of his adversaries in debate to such an extent as to make their arguments almost his own. For the professional man there should be no nobler aim than to emulate this example; for the directors of economic policy it should be a pragmatic imperative.

To settle a problem of policy, to settle on a particular kind of policy for one or another subject, inevitably means discussion and dispute among interested partners. It would therefore seem natural if first we were to clarify the essential facts and the background history of the issue; and if, next, we were to look for a few basic aims and purposes on which the partners might be able to agree. The more specific these aims are, the better the prospect for an early and realistic solution. And realistic in this context means, almost always, reasonable; for it is only if all partners feel that their interests have been taken into account that a more than ephemeral compact can be established.

Once agreement on basic facts and aims is reached, the partners in search of a policy can confine further work to the discussion of the means for achieving the agreed aims. True, this is not all as simple as it sounds: It takes wisdom and discipline, it takes an erudite group of negotiators to carry out this idea. It is also clear that among the basic aims may have to be included certain characteristics to which the means themselves might have to conform or which they might have to avoid. Nevertheless, it is likely that a concrete content for international arrangements on agricultural policies and trade will best be developed from a recognized set of facts and from a general philosophy and broad principles and aims that follow from it, and that this sequence will also be the most effective approach to actual negotiation of such arrangements: first to discuss and agree on general aims and principles, and to be firmly guided by these standards and rules in the subsequent negotiation of the details of implementation. This, then, is the general idea and pattern to which the present study aims to conform.

Before we can formulate concrete suggestions for international arrangements on agricultural policies and trade, we must travel a considerable distance over familiar and not so familiar ground in order to gain a sufficiently extensive view of the scene with which we are to deal. For this journey, the reader's patience as well as attention are herewith invited.

J. H. RICHTER

Beech Hill
McLean, Virginia
January, 1964

Contents

Agricultural Protection and Trade

1. Agriculture in an Industrial Setting

WHEN WE think about the problem of agricultural trade and look for solutions, we must first inquire into its nature and genesis. Because of low farm incomes and increasing prosperity in other segments of their economies, industrial countries were not only inclined, but also could afford, to extend special income protection to their agricultures. These policies have, in turn, affected international trade and world prices of agricultural products through the corollary measures that both importing and some exporting countries have applied toward the outside world.

Agriculture in an expanding industrial economy labors under several major handicaps. Demand for its products does not increase greatly in such a society. Income and price elasticities of demand are low, in some cases zero, and in many such areas population growth is also low. Much of the increase in consumer expenditures on food is absorbed by the built-in services the consumer buys, on an increasing scale, with his better-packaged, -preserved, and -prepared daily food.

On the other hand, agriculture not only profits but also suffers from rapid progress in technology, which, in turn, is driven on by the quick pace of economic development in industry. Technical progress and innovation inevitably invade agriculture as well, but, as in industry, they can raise productivity and income only if the new or improved resources can be fully, or nearly fully, employed. However, and contrary to the situation in industry with its much higher demand elasticities, such increases in economic productivity and income, with full employment of the improved resources, can only come about if prices are not pushed down—that is to say, if output is not, or not significantly, raised. And this, in turn, would call for a displacement of agricultural labor, either on the individual farms, or through shifts in output from some farms to others or even as between countries, at a pace which is socially or politically intolerable or impracticable. Yet, without such displacement, productivity in agriculture may increase only little, or may even decline, with corresponding repercussions—if not on farm income directly (because of government aid), then on the nation's income in the aggregate.

The millions of independent agricultural producers for once fulfill here the postulate of theory regarding competition: Each farm's market contribution is so small that any change a farmer makes in his dispositions cannot affect prices. Hence, when production has begun to increase because of technological progress, the individual farmer is powerless to stem the tide of price decline; his position would only become worse were he to curtail his own output. It is in this context that farmers have largely come to depend on government for income protection, demand supplementation (surplus disposal), and supply adjustment that they cannot accomplish for themselves as easily as can industrial producers acting either individually or in concert. Unguided, they push on and increase market output; with price elasticities of demand below 1, total receipts decline in the face of unchanged or even increased outlays on input items, taxes, and interest. In the wake of improved technology, the stage thus is set for successive self-defeating waves of increases in output and reductions in income. It is in this roundabout fashion that the wholesome force of technical progress contributes to the problem of agriculture in the industrial world.*

The problem is, of course, not insoluble; it is essentially one of slow mobility of resources that, I believe, will gradually pervade other segments of our Western civilization as well. Such a development is merely the expression of a more civilized set of values in the life of the common man; and the problems it raises are only the expression of a more humane approach of society in dealing with it.

Governments do realize that a fundamental correction of the present income problem in agriculture can only come through improvement in the efficiency of resource utilization, and that such improvement is tantamount to a further reduction in the input of resources employed to bring about a given level of output. For all practical purposes, this means a further reduction in the farm population.

In most countries, such reductions have already reached formidable proportions. In the United States and Germany, the agricultural population, between 1947 and 1960, declined from around 18 to below 10 per cent of the total population. In the United Kingdom, the decline was from 6 to 4.5 per cent; in France, from 30 to 23 per cent. Despite its extraordinary extent, this shift does not seem to have been sufficiently extensive to prevent the gap between agricultural and nonagricultural incomes from widening still further. Special programs are therefore needed for the support of farm income to permit gradual adjustment and to meet the demand for an assured minimum standard of living, without obliging—as most programs do—"the bene-

* Additional factors or characteristics that distinguish agriculture's problems of production and marketing from those in other industries are well described in G. Hallet and G. James, *Farming for Consumers*, "Hobart Paper No. 22" (London: Institute of Economic Affairs, 1963), p. 15 f.

ficiary to produce unwanted output in order to qualify" for support.*

Beyond that, it is quite obvious that there are goals and tenets of public policy that set limits to the extent to which the craving for productivity can be given rein at the expense of other interests of society at large. In many industrial areas of the world, the dilemma will perhaps be solved by more appropriate "town-and-country planning" that will reconcile activities designed further to improve standards of material well-being with measures to retain, or regain, other values, such as more recreation and living space for the industrial population and more cultural amenities for the rural people.

Such an approach is embodied in the longer-range goals of farm policies in several countries in their programs for rural development, adjustment of agricultural structures, and industrial decentralization. In quite a number of countries, including the EEC—Italy, France, Germany, and Benelux—sizable progress in this direction has already been made. This integration of agricultural policy with general and regional economic policy has gone forward under very deliberate legislative and administrative efforts, one of its central goals being the creation for agriculturists of nonagricultural employment possibilities in the vicinity of their accustomed homes. The ill effects of labor's immobility are thus being mitigated by greater mobility of capital. The investments in infrastructure needed in such regions are borne by governments or by mixed government-private enterprises (for example, the French Sociétés d'Economie Mixte).†

---

* E. F. Nash, "Agriculture and the Common Market," in *Journal of Agricultural Economics* (Reading, England), May, 1962.

† An instructive review of measures taken and progress achieved with respect to such policies of regional agricultural-industrial development is to be found in an article by T. Dams, "Industrie-Ansiedlung in Ländlichen Entwicklungsräumen," in *Agrarwirtschaft* (Hanover), September, 1963.

2. Agricultural Support in the World at Large

THE POSITION of agriculture in the industrial countries thus presents problems of a special type. But there are agricultural problems in other countries as well.

Let us first consider agriculture in the strictly agricultural and the less developed countries. There are certainly great problems there, but they are of a different type. They are easy to understand if they are obviously due to artificially stimulated expansion of output in countries that might be customers. They are also easy to understand if obviously due to the corollary circumstances of economic and social backwardness, or poverty, or to the impediments to economic development that, in the guise of backwardness, are unavoidable in a social and spiritual setting whose values, standards, and rules are vastly different from our own.*

* It is because of such differences that some of us have strong reservations about the sweeping assumptions that are often made regarding the desirable and possible type and pace of "economic development" for these different societies. In Max Weber's view, "the dominance of magic . . . has been one of the greatest impediments to the rationalization of economic life." (*Wirtschaftsgeschichte*, Munich, 1924, p. 308.) An instructive review of the great variety of problems that we face with respect to "progress" in those societies may be found in the proceedings of a seminar held in July, 1953, in Gonville and Caius College, Cambridge, England (made possible by a Rockefeller Foundation grant), and published in A. Leslie Banks (ed.), *The Development of Tropical and Sub-Tropical Countries* (London, 1954). This is a splendid example of the rich intellectual productiveness of the British "round-table" custom if supported, as it was in this case, by experts of great experience and learning in their respective fields, drawing their expertise largely from long years of work in the areas concerned.

7

And, indeed, these two broad influences actually account for most of the farm problems in these two groups of countries. Their governments can do little to alleviate them by measures tantamount to income transfers in favor of agriculture, since agriculture itself is either the mainstay of the national income or a very large contributor to it. Often, far from being supported by other segments of the economy, its own revenue is being drawn upon to help finance industrial and economic development.

Second, with respect to agriculture in the Communist or centrally planned and directed economies, the root of its problems is also clear: Under deliberate policies for rapid economic development, attended by much misdirection and waste, huge resources were extorted from agriculture and the agricultural population for this very purpose. Also, and partly because of this policy, agriculture had to operate with insufficient economic incentives and insufficient investment, to the detriment of productivity. To the extent that these policies have in recent years been modified, improvements in the agricultural situation have been recorded.*

To cover the various systems or measures of agricultural support in a broad sweep, I should perhaps say that, as far as the Western countries are concerned, their policies aim mainly at increasing per capita farm income, though in the process they often cannot avoid increasing total agricultural output as well. To be effective, the policies must overcome deficiencies in natural, economic, and human

* It is perhaps strange that I should mention this advance at a time when large food-import demand by the Communist area testifies to the failures of their agricultural policies. But we must not forget that, although improvements were inadequate, they were not entirely absent; that failures here were offset by improvements there; and that, over and above the temporary influence of a very bad growing season, there may be forces at work gradually transforming some of the agricultural-surplus areas into industrial food-deficit regions.

resources that may impede progress toward those aims. The countries' policies thus appear as efforts to offset or to correct such drawbacks; usually they are a mixture of both. The "offsetting" type is more protectionist in character, not too much concerned if output is expanded even beyond reasonable expectations regarding sales possibilities. The "correcting" type is more forward-looking and mainly directed toward raising per capita income and productivity and maintaining trade.

In the underdeveloped countries, largely producers of primary products, policy goals must prominently include (as a priority aim) the increase in total output, both in order to increase and improve domestic food supplies for rapidly growing populations and to maintain or increase export income and raw-material supplies for expanding domestic industries. Similar goals prevail in the Communist countries, though progress toward their achievement is often hampered by the pursuit of other economic and political goals.

In the Western countries, price and income supports for agriculture are rather general, though there are exceptions —i.e., countries with fewer and more reluctantly imposed controls. The price and income programs are protected by import controls such as high tariffs, variable import levies, and quantitative restrictions, government trading, and quasi trade monopolies. Export subsidies and special trade arrangements with customer or supplier countries, government purchase and storage operations and operations by marketing organizations with statutory powers, and special schemes for surplus disposal at home and abroad are also important.

In the United Kingdom, direct producer subsidies (deficiency payments) are the main form of agricultural support. Subsidies for small farms or those in unfavorable

locations are granted in a number of countries, while subsidies for such input items as fertilizer, machinery, and
motor fuel are widely applied. In some cases, consumer
subsidies are given to offset the effect of high farm prices or
as an alternative to producer subsidies.

These and other measures are, in part, used not only to
improve the immediate price and market situation for
agriculture, but also to assist more basic, structural
improvements in production, transportation, and distribution. Land reclamation and resettlement, regional development projects including industrial decentralization, consolidation of holdings into units that can be operated
economically, with efficient layout of buildings, are among
such improvements. Most of these basic agricultural-sup-
port measures, however, are still in their infancy.

Finally, we need to mention the special services for
agriculture in the form of farm credit, education, and research. These are, for the most part, historic services that
have a long tradition, especially in the developed countries.
They are not, and have not been, without effect upon
agricultural output and efficiency, the development of surpluses, and the like.

There are some students of present farm problems who
call attention to the extent of government efforts to develop and promote research, paid from public funds, designed for application in the production, marketing, and
utilization of agricultural commodities. They maintain
that the results of this research have been much more effective in stimulating production than consumption, and
that these techniques are placed, free of charge, at the disposal of farmers who already produce more than is salable.

This is a problem that has to be faced. It should be
recognized, however, that research contributes primarily to
increased *efficiency* of production, rather than to increased

production as such. Furthermore, it would seem strange if governments promoting scientific work for agriculture would deliberately curb the pursuit of knowledge in order to help redress the balance between supply and requirements for farm products. Research addresses itself to humanity's basic need for knowledge, including knowledge of how our material and cultural requirements can be filled with less effort so as to allow a wider diffusion of the amenities of life. The question must be weighed in this context as well; and agricultural development in the needy areas, where expansion of production is absolutely essential, will no doubt profit considerably from the achievements of past and future research. We must not forget, however, that practical results depend much less on further research than on the application of past research findings to the daily routine on farms.

3. Agriculture in GATT

FACED WITH the problems described, the governments of the industrialized countries have, during the past fifteen years, found it difficult, or been altogether unable or unwilling, to apply to agricultural trade the basic rules of the General Agreement on Tariffs and Trade (GATT). On the other hand, the agricultural exporting countries have insisted that certain GATT rules at least should govern agricultural trade as well.

The complaint that the General Agreement, administered by the GATT Secretariat in Geneva, has not been successful in preventing an increase in agricultural protectionism thus has a long history. Protectionism in the importing countries has gradually grown under special measures for the protection of balances of payments. Later, when balances of payments had recovered sufficient equilibrium to go without such protection, no significant liberalization of import policies was recorded, and the call for recognition of agriculture's special situation and of a special deal for agriculture became louder and more insistent. GATT itself, shot through as it is with exceptions, exemptions, and loopholes, made possible the use of subterfuges without formal violation of its rules. These loopholes also permitted some exporting countries to protect, on the trade side, their domestic support programs and to maintain their exports (by import quotas and export subsidies).

There are, above all, GATT's provisions permitting state trading. Countries hard-pressed by GATT for liberalization could, at any time, put sensitive commodities under state trading and thus secure the most complete protection. It need only be remembered that there is a very small gap between that which some countries now have and full state trading—a practice, moreover, which in importing countries can be made quite unbureaucratic and confined to the easy license and skimming procedures that existed under the German import and stocking agencies (handled by just a handful of people). Then there is the Torquay Protocol of April 21, 1951 (I [a] [ii]), under which countries must conform to Part II of the General Agreement only to the extent that compliance is not inconsistent with their own legislation existing on April 21, 1951. It is under this article that Germany justified the quantitative regulation it exercised through the import and stocking agencies. Furthermore, there is GATT's Article XI, specifically permitting quantitative trade restrictions on agricultural products necessary to enforce such government-support programs as provide for domestic restriction (of undefined effectiveness) on output or marketing. There is, finally, Article XXV, Section 5, under which the Contracting Parties of GATT may and do waive obligations imposed upon member countries; since most governments are always under pressure from special interests, they are usually somewhat sympathetic to similar problems in other countries and tend to be lenient with respect to "waivers" on the basis of a give-and-take attitude.

It was in this climate and in this situation that pressures for the elaboration of a Special GATT Code for Agriculture have been building up. Countries that favored the idea were found on both sides of the fence.

Led by the Common Market governments, the provisions of GATT were re-examined by the Contracting Parties six years ago in the light of the agricultural policies that had become ingrained in the attitudes of many countries. At the 13th Session of GATT, the German Minister of Agriculture declared that the GATT was outmoded so far as agricultural products are concerned and that a separate Code for Agriculture—practically exempting agricultural producers from the provisions of GATT—should be written into this international agreement. The representative of the EEC Commission, knowing that shortly they would write a special code of their own, also advocated a special Code for Agriculture. German compromise proposals at that time suggested that each country retain its own market regulations and price structures indefinitely.

The Swiss made the point that GATT had exceptions for underdeveloped countries and that agriculture should be treated in a similar way. The Austrians reportedly said that if GATT gave them too much trouble on agriculture, they were indeed ready to put all agricultural products under state trading. Practically all other countries outside the main exporter group contended that some special framework for agriculture would indeed be a good idea. And the more detached professional observers contended that, through its special status under the existing GATT rules and practices, agriculture in effect had had a special code ever since the inception of the General Agreement.

While specialists in a number of places continued to look askance at the Special Code idea, their governments, in pursuit of loftier policies, had already administered the *coup de grâce* to all opposition: In March, 1962, the Contracting Parties of GATT virtually gave their blessing to the European Economic Community's so-called Common Agricultural Policy by concluding the negotiations under GATT's Article XXIV and thus accepting the EEC's economic union as a *fait accompli.**

* That there have been a number of joint declarations by the EEC and agricultural exporting countries indicating intentions for further negotiations on certain issues does not alter the fact that the GATT community, despite some strong rhetorical declarations, at that time

The very idea of the EEC's Common Agricultural Policy is, of course, nothing but a special code for agriculture. This code, unilaterally imposed, provides for protection over a wide area of agricultural products that cannot, through GATT, be limited by negotiated bindings at this time and under present practice. The EEC's variable import levies, minimum import prices, preferences for associated territories, and quantitative emergency restrictions are cases in point.

A special code of this sort is, of course, a far cry from what might be reasonably envisaged as an adjustment of GATT rules to take account of the special situation of agriculture that has been pointed out. Such an adjustment would preserve an international rule of conduct for agriculture as well, whereas the special code, if unadjusted, would altogether remove agricultural policy from any kind of international discipline.

It should be recorded here, for what it may be worth, that it was S. L. Mansholt, the EEC's Vice-President and Commissioner for Agriculture, who expressed a desire for "a code of good behavior in agricultural policy" to emerge from the forthcoming negotiations in GATT as an integral part of the so-called Kennedy Round.[*]

---

signed its capitulation. Although those who were thus beaten at the 1961–62 GATT game do not like to admit it, this is the general interpretation of the outcome of the Article XXIV/6 negotiations. So shrewd an observer as W. Zeller, the Brussels correspondent of the *Neue Zürcher Zeitung*, confirms that "the conclusion of those negotiations under Article XXIV, Paragraph 6, of GATT is interpreted as an international acceptance of the common EEC tariff and of the agricultural variable levy system." (Evening ed., September 13, 1963, Blatt 3; author's translation.)

[*] *Foreign Agriculture*, April 22, 1963, p. 15. Note, however, the Commission's later proposal on how to negotiate in GATT (see p. 90 ff.), which is not exactly an application of this idea.

4. Agriculture in the EEC

WHILE THE problem of reconciling the need for farm support with the need for maintaining agricultural trade has been developing over a number of years, its great significance was suddenly high-lighted by the formation of the European Economic Community and the agricultural policy the Community proposes to pursue. The whole issue was brought to a head by the EEC's vigorous steps toward integration and its unbending attitude in the GATT negotiations of 1960–62. Clearly, special arrangements, special efforts to safeguard agricultural trade with the EEC, had become necessary. And clearly, also (although some countries flirted with the idea of separate understandings with the EEC), such efforts would have to aim at world-wide arrangements. For it was obvious that the importance of the EEC in the world's commercial agricultural trade would be extraordinary.*

* For a terse summation of the present need for reasonable world-wide negotiations, see Roger Savary's article "EEC in the World," in *World Agriculture,* October, 1962. The case for a revision of GATT in the sense of a reasonable code for agriculture is well made in Eric Wyndham White's address delivered at the Annual Meeting of the Finnish Foreign Trade Association, Helsinki, on May 8, 1962. Statements made with reference to the Brussels negotiations between the EEC and the U.K. emphasize the world-wide character of arrangements envisioned in their negotiations. Cf. the communiqué issued by the Commonwealth Prime Ministers upon conclusion of their conference in London on September 19, 1962. Also cf. EEC President Hallstein's reference in his address at Lincoln, Nebraska, December 6, 1962, when he confirmed that the "Commission has already made proposals for such world-wide agreements" in the negotiations with the British. Similarly, there have been many other acknowledgments of the need for a world-wide approach: the plans advanced by the French Ministers Pisani and Baumgartner, statements by

In order to throw more light on the basic conditions and policies with which such international arrangements would have to cope, it may be useful first to review the essence and then the details of the agricultural provisions that the EEC has planned or promulgated.*

The need for a special EEC policy for agriculture and agricultural products, in contrast to industrial products, had been clear from the outset. It was generally understood, however, that these special provisions would aim at nothing more than the establishment of procedures that would allow internal market unification to develop more gradually than in the case of industrial products, and outsiders were assured that no increase in external protection was intended.

Vice-President Mansholt of the EEC Commission, and, for example, the remarks made by Drs. H. B. Krohn and Günther Schmitt of the EEC in their monograph *Agrarpolitik für Europa* (Special issue No. 15 of *Agrarwirtschaft*, Hanover, 1962), pp. 144–46. Many others could be cited.

* For a number of sidelights and more complete information, see the excellent paper by the late Professor E. F. Nash on "Agriculture and the Common Market," published in the *Journal of Agricultural Economics*, May, 1962. Also see FAO's Commodity Policy Study 13 (1962), prepared under the direction of Gerda Blau; Max Börlin, "Die Agrarintegration der EWG und die Schweiz," in *Aussenwirtschaft* (Zurich), No. 2–3, 1962; E. W. Learn, "Common Market Grain Policies," in *Foreign Agricultural Trade of the United States*, USDA, January, 1963; and J. H. Richter, "Agricultural Policy in the European Common Market," in *The Journal of Farm Economics*, August, 1961; and "A Note on Agriculture in the Common Market," in *Kyklos*, XIV (1961), Fasc. 3. Details are, of course, given in various publications of the EEC Commission in Brussels, especially since the decisions of January 14, 1962 (briefly reviewed in a release by the Foreign Agricultural Service, datelined Washington, D.C., February 7, 1962). Special aspects are treated in altogether outstanding studies by Professors Hanau, Plate, and Woermann, and by Drs. Grupe and Krohn, in *Agrarwirtschaft*, especially the issues of June, 1958; October, 1960; February, 1962; and May, 1962; also see *Flugschriften der DLG*, XXIX, Frankfurt/Main, 1959. The best up-to-date description and explanation of the EEC's agricultural policy and its practical application will be found in W. Zeller's article "Die EWG Agrarpolitik in der Praxis," in *Neue Zürcher Zeitung*, September 1, 1963, Blatt 10; September 2, noon ed., September 4, evening ed., Blatt 3; and September 13, evening ed., Blatt 3.

Since the publication on June 30, 1960, of the EEC Commission's proposals for a Common Agricultural Policy, and especially since the decisions on variable levies of January 14, 1962, it had become clear that under the order actually envisaged, it would be difficult to negotiate limits to EEC protection in GATT as now written or practiced. There will be such a system of variable import levies. Quantitative restrictions may also apply. There will be preferences for overseas or associated territories. For some of those agricultural commodities for which fixed tariffs are proposed, special market regulations with minimum import prices are envisioned. It is likely that output of some products will be stimulated by high producer prices protected by such measures, with resultant reduction in imports. Even burdensome "surpluses" may arise; subsidies are proposed for their disposal at home and abroad.

For the time being, no agreement has been reached by the member governments with respect to price levels. But political pressures have made it obvious that it will be most difficult to avoid an increase precisely in areas where expansion of output is most feasible and likely. In these circumstances, the envisioned producer-price unification as such has a built-in tendency toward increased protection, expansion of output, and reduction of imports or even "surplus" production.

With support prices for important agricultural products thus to be maintained at predetermined high levels regardless of price competition from "outside" suppliers, imports are possible only after domestic supplies are disposed of. Within an individual country framework, this system has existed before the EEC was formed. However, its extension to the member countries taken as a unit precludes trade of outside suppliers until *all* EEC producers have (to put it crudely) disposed of their produce, either within their own countries or in the other countries of the Union.*

The maintenance of predetermined levels of high support prices that cannot be influenced by competition from either "outside" or other "inside" suppliers has another special significance for evaluation of the EEC's agricultural policy as an ingredient of economic union. A true economic or customs union is based upon the idea that productivity gains will come from a relocation of economic pursuits toward a more economical pattern *within* the union area. An industry or product here will gain at the expense of an industry or product there, and another industry there will gain at the expense of an industry here, with all of them taken together coming out with a net gain in the process, because precisely this process implies an increase in total productivity. The true customs union thus aims, in the first place, to gain from shifts *within* the union area, not at the expense of third countries.†

The situation in the EEC is different. We know that, in agriculture, increased prices readily tend to call forth increased production. We also know that reduced prices do not as readily, or not at all, result in reduced production—notably if the predetermined support-price levels are high.

---

* The difference between a consolidated area policy and the sum total of separate individual country policies in the area with respect to restraints on policies leading to expansion of output is eloquently described in Lawrence B. Krause's study published in *Factors Affecting the U.S. Balance of Payments* (Joint Economic Committee, 87th Cong., 2d sess., Washington, D.C., 1962); see especially p. 121. This point was overlooked by U.S. negotiator W. M. Blumenthal when he expressed the view that "it is far from certain that we would be better off under six separate restrictive schemes than under the single system which is being put into effect." (From his address at the Agricultural Outlook Conference, Washington, D.C., November 13, 1962; according to *Bulletin from the European Community*, December, 1962, Washington, D.C.)

† It is true, of course, that it may also gain at the expense of potential imports, but only insofar as this is brought about by an increase in intra-area productivity, with resultant price pressure.

5. The Agricultural Policy of the EEC

THE CONCEPT of a Common Agricultural Policy (CAP) for the member countries of the European Economic Community has been laid down in Articles 38–47 of the Treaty of Rome of March 25, 1957—EEC's basic charter. Details of this concept were modified and interpreted in subsequent negotiations among the member countries in accordance with ideas largely proposed by the EEC's Executive, the Commission, and approved unanimously by the Council of the Ministers of the individual member states.

The common agricultural policy of the EEC is still in the making. It is to traverse a preparatory period of gradual introduction before it takes full effect on January 1, 1970. Its aims emerged largely from past policies and principles pursued in the individual member countries and were further developed or modified by the Commission under the overriding idea of economic union and integration. These aims may be stated as follows:

1. To create a common market in which agricultural trade moves under conditions that correspond to conditions in a fully integrated national market, especially with respect to prices, and in which policies affecting supply, demand, and trade, despite great emphasis on the direct support of EEC agriculture, are governed by rational and realistic concepts.

2. To raise farm incomes through these market policies, but, with emphasis on "family farms," also through agricul-

tural policies of "structural" improvement and general policies of regional economic development.*

In pursuance of these aims, the EEC's Common Agricultural Policy conceives of two main categories of approach —a policy of structural adjustments† and a market and price policy.‡ These two main categories are supplemented by more general provisions on social policy concerning freedom of movement of labor and settlement in agriculture, under certain conditions, as between member countries; social security; and professional training.§

Policy on "Structure"

One of the features of the EEC's agricultural-policy blueprint more reasonable and encouraging to economic interests in "outside countries" is the aim of long-term structural adjustment. Theoretically, this part of the policy is to be as basic as is the part on market and price measures (to be described below). Land consolidation, melioration, farm credit, technical training, help for shifts out of marginal farms, withdrawal of unsuitable land from agricultural uses, and a regional development policy with industrial decentralization and the creation of jobs in industry and services in farming areas—all of these are essential in the plans of the EEC Commission and in the programs of member governments.

---

* This is an adaptation of the version of basic principles "devised by the EEC Commission and approved by the Council," as stated in Krohn and Schmitt, *Agrarpolitik für Europa* (see p. 92). The present author believes that the above represents fairly what is stated in official documents and what has transpired through official pronouncements by Commission members and in member countries over the past few years.

† Rome Treaty, Article 39, and Proposals of the Commission for coordination of structural policies.

‡ Rome Treaty, Articles 40 and 43, and, especially, twelve ordinances promulgated on January 14 (April 4), 1962. See below.

§ Rome Treaty, Articles 41, 48 ff., and 117 ff.

The *initiative* for measures of structural reform (and, of course, their execution) lies with the individual member governments. The Commission, however, has the right to make pertinent proposals, and the obligation to assist in the community-wide coordination of such reforms. Community help in financing structural measures is also provided for.*

In its explanatory memorandum introducing proposals made by it to the Council concerning the coordination of policies on agricultural structure, the Commission reiterates its belief that the aims of the CAP cannot be realized by market and price policies alone, and that an improvement in farm incomes depends mainly on improvements of the structure of agriculture.

The proposed Council "Decision" provides for an inventory, in each member state, of all structural measures now in force and for current notifications to the Commission of measures to be taken in the future. It also is to provide for the establishment of a committee of representatives of the member states (and of the Commission) to discuss the countries' policies and measures in this field and to assist in the coordination and scrutiny of these policies.†

It is in the nature of the subject that in terms of practical measures, structural reform has not yet received as much attention nor as much detailed study for implementation as have market and price policies. And it is human nature first to grapple with those problems that

---

* The European Adjustment and Guaranty Fund, created by the EEC Council as a general tool for the collection and disbursement of finances for the EEC's agricultural policy, is to devote part of its receipts to financing structural measures in individual member countries. ("Verordnung über die Finanzierung der Gemeinsamen Agrarpolitik," *Amtsblatt der Europäischen Gemeinschaften,* April 20, 1962.)

† Supplement to the *Bulletin of the EEC,* No. 3, March, 1962.

require immediate decisions and to go slow on those of a more long-term character. Yet it is somewhat disquieting that the proposed Council "Decision" has not thus far been adopted or otherwise acted upon, although the Commission's draft dates back to September 20, 1961, and was published in March, 1962.

No executive ordinances have thus as yet appeared with respect to this chapter of the Common Agricultural Policy that ought to be the most important. Conversely, a flood of rules and regulations has been put into effect for most of the protectionist market and price policy. In fairness it must be remembered, however, that so far as the Commission itself is concerned, its proposals and comments on structural reform show that basically it acknowledges the need for contemplating the problem of agriculture with reason and economic common sense.

Market and Price Policy

A quick orientation with respect to the technical content of the EEC's market and price policies is afforded by the decisions arrived at by the Council of Ministers on January 14, 1962, following a debate that lasted four weeks and caused the physical collapse of one member and the exhaustion of all others.*

* The twelve Ordinances and Decisions then promulgated and finally dated April 4, 1962, were published in the *Amtsblatt der Europäischen Gemeinschaften* of April 20, 1962; they regulate the gradual introduction of common-market organizations for grains, poultry and eggs, pork, wine, fruit and vegetables, and decree the adoption, as from July 1, 1962 (later postponed to July 30, 1962) of a system of variable import levies for grains, pork, poultry, and eggs. Principles for the regulation of the market for sugar, milk and milk products, beef and rice, subject to early specification with or without variable levies, were also included. There are only a few agricultural commodities for which the Rome Treaty foresaw fixed or zero tariffs (some of which in the meantime are threatened by the variable-levy idea), for example, tobacco, cotton, fruits and vegetables, oilseeds, and vegetable oils.

However, for the type of discussion I wish to consider here, such a technical review would not suffice. We must also address ourselves to the ideas underlying EEC policy if we are to gain an insight into its logic and structure.

Inherent in the concept of a common market is, of course, the creation of one unified whole out of the individual national markets of the member countries. This is a commonplace goal, so to speak, for a common-market effort. It may be taken for granted. And it determines many of the techniques that must be employed. It does not, however, represent a basic philosophy of how agriculture is to be supported in the field of markets and prices.

In the EEC, such a basic philosophy might be described as one of *strategic price stabilization;* its core is the price stabilization of a strategic group of commodities whose price level pervades agriculture as a whole and determines land values as much as opportunity costs of alternative lines of production and utilization of output. With import protection being considerable and domestic demand slowly rising, such a policy is, thus, on the proceeds side, the main determinant of total farm income, at least in the central sector of grain-livestock farming that constitutes the principal problem area in agriculture.*

The strategic group of commodities I am talking about is made up of *grains, sugar, and milk.* These are products whose production and, partly, consumption are rather inelastic with respect to price changes. Price changes for

---

* This is the context that explains why it is wrong to claim that there is free price formation and market operation for most products, and that price supports and deliberate market management, with or without quantitative controls, are confined to a limited group of commodities. Such claims are, wrongly, made both in the EEC and in the United States. Also, under conditions of mixed farming—and quite aside from the context described above—income transfers for the benefit of any one agricultural sector almost invariably constitute support for agriculture as a whole.

these products do not therefore have much corrective impact upon supply and demand; and variations in the latter could thus result in extraordinary fluctuations in prices and incomes. Furthermore, fully 50 per cent of EEC's plowland is in grains, and the output of grains and sugarbeets (including potatoes, whose returns in food and feed use are largely determined by grain prices) accounts for one-half of the total value of farm production; and milk is the most important item in the cash income of the needy small farmer.

With a considerable degree of logic, therefore, the EEC's market policy provides for price stability for these commodities under a system of "target" prices and so-called support or "intervention" prices (the price level at which the authorities must intervene in the market if prices tend to fall below the support levels). The target prices for wholesale parity are set from year to year. Actual market prices, and hence producer prices, move somewhere between the target and the intervention levels. The spread between these two levels is to amount to from 5 to 10 per cent; for grains in Germany, in the 1963–64 season, it is about 7 per cent.*

This system, in turn, is secured by what amounts to fixed import prices—called "threshold" prices (*Schwellenpreise, prix de seuil*)—which are derived from the target prices in a relationship that is to make it possible for the market to approximate the target prices. (In Germany, for example, the basic target price for wheat for July, 1963, was $118.88 per 1,000 kg, protected by a threshold price of $119.50.†

The difference between any c.i.f. import purchase price

---

* Alfred C. Toepfer, *Die deutsche Getreidemarktordnung in der EWG 1963–64* (Hamburg, August, 1963).

† *Ibid.*, p. 7.

and the threshold price is imposed upon the former as an import levy, and to the extent that the prices at which shipments are offered free frontier vary, that levy also varies: thus, the basic tool of the system—for the target-price commodities and insofar as there are still sizable import needs—is the *variable import levy*.

As long as there is no unified price level throughout the EEC countries, the target prices and, hence, the threshold prices among the member states must differ, since they have to protect different producer-price levels. Therefore, the variable import levies of the member states also differ, and such levies are even applied to trade among themselves, although, of course, only to the extent of the difference between each exporting member country's free-frontier offer price and the respective importing member country's threshold price. There is also a small intra-area preference margin (in the case of grains at present about 1 per cent) by which the threshold price for imports from member countries (and hence the variable import levy) is reduced, as against the threshold price for imports from third countries.*

* I believe that the importance of the differential treatment of imports from member countries as against those from third countries has not found sufficient attention. As such, the present preferential margin in the threshold price (about 1 per cent in the case of grains) is small. But this fact must not make us forget the great advantage now accruing to exporting member countries on their exports to other members. Since the beginning of the variable-levy regime on July 30, 1962, member countries have been able to export to other members at their domestic prices, whereas previously exports (even to member countries) had to be at much lower "world" prices, or not much above them. It is true, of course, that this advantage can only be realized to the extent that exports to other member countries actually take place; it is also true that the inducement to buy from other members rather than from third countries still depends upon that (at present small) preferential margin in the threshold price. Yet this margin is to increase gradually, and to the extent necessary to promote progressively intracommunity trade. (Articles 9 and 26 of EEC Regulation No. 19, of April 4, 1962.) Margins for 1963–64 have already been increased and may take only a small further increase to create enough of a pull

As price levels become gradually unified in EEC, the "internal" variable levies must gradually disappear, since their equalizing function will of course cease to be needed as prices become equalized. For the time being, no agreement has been reached by the member governments with respect to common price levels for the target-price commodities.

As far as *meat and eggs* are concerned, some freedom of price formation in EEC markets is to be retained, although regulatory devices, as we shall see, are important. Again, there is logic in the retention of greater market freedom for these commodities, since in their case elasticities of demand as well as supply, under European conditions, are still considerable.

For *poultry meat, pork, and eggs*—and grain is a highly important component in the total feed used for their production—import protection at the frontier includes an element representing the incidence on feeding costs of the difference between feed-grain prices in the importing member state and the exporting member state (or, for third-country exports, the world-market price). This element represents only cost equalization (if calculated correctly) and gives no protection to the "feed converter" as such, though if he produces his own grain for feed, it extends to him, as grain producer, the same protection as given other grain producers who sell their grain as feed. Again, with

toward purchases from other members. This factor needs careful watching and handling just because it is of no immediate practical importance, considering the outturn of European crops in 1963. It is also interesting to note how such advantages accruing to exporting members will gradually become expensive to importing member countries. The advantages, and the corollary expense, far from touching the accounts of the participating *individual* businesses, will find their expression in the government budgets and *national* accounts of the countries concerned. If the EEC Commission proposals of November 5, 1963, for immediate grain-price unification are accepted, these effects will even be more drastic.

gradual equalization of feed-grain prices as between member states, this differential will become zero in trade among member countries.

There is, however, an additional—fixed—tariff serving as direct "converter" protection. This fixed-tariff element is to be applied toward third countries only and represents the preference for intra-area trading; it began as a modest 2 per cent (from July 30, 1962), now is 3 per cent, and is to reach the full 7 per cent of the common external tariff upon completion of the common market for these products in 1970. In the intermediate period prior to 1970, both imports from third countries *and* those from member countries must also pay the tariff hitherto imposed upon imports by the individual member countries, gradually to be reduced, and disappearing with completion of the common market.

Finally, for each of these products the Council of Ministers may and does set so-called minimum import prices (sluice-gate prices, *Einschleusungspreise, prix d'écluse*) for imports from *third* countries—in the case of pork also for imports from *member* countries. These minimum import prices are to be enforced by "supplementary" variable levies—a provision theoretically to be invoked only "if the world price becomes abnormally low," but actually applied contrary to this rule.*

---

* See Articles 7, 6, and 6 of EEC Council Regulations Nos. 20, 21, and 22, respectively, adopted on January 14, 1962, and dated April 4, 1962. It is important to note that these provisions were before the members of GATT when they negotiated and sealed their accommodation with the EEC in the spring of 1962. The negotiators in GATT must, as a result, have been under the impression that sluice-gate prices (and, hence, the pertinent supplementary levies) would only be invoked in accordance with the spirit of the anti-dumping and emergency rules of GATT's Articles VI and XIX. An especially flagrant case of violation on the part of the EEC is that of the minimum import price for chicken meat. Such minimum import prices have, allegedly, been decreed "to avoid market disturb-

In order to give an idea of how the various elements of import protection shape up, I shall specify an example for poultry meat in Germany (U.S. cents per lb.), October, 1963:*

1. Lowest third-country invoice price c.i.f. Germany	30.90
2. "Supplementary" levy (to enforce gate price)	1.70
3. Minimum import (or gate) price	32.60
4. Feed-cost equalization (variable levy)	6.60
5. Fixed tariff ("converter" protection, which at the same time represents an intra-area preference), now 3 per cent, to reach 7 per cent upon full integration	0.98
6. Fixed tariff (holdover from pre-variable-levy period; now about 9 per cent, to decline to zero by 1970)	2.97
7. Total third-country price c.i.f. Germany (levy-paid)	43.05

Member-country exports to Germany (or any other member) do not pay items (2) and (5); thus, item (3) does not apply to them. Also, item (4) is less to the extent that differences in the price of feed grains between member countries are less. Disregarding this latter point, since it concerns only differences in costs, it can be said that member-country exports to Germany can now enter at a total charge (excluding feed equalization) of 2.97 cents per lb., com-

---

ances." But they are being applied only toward *third* countries whose prices do not threaten such disturbances, whereas they are absent in the case of exports from other EEC *member* countries whose export prices, under the impact of large government export subsidies (France and Belgium), have in fact been reduced to dumping levels. It is a mystery why, in the "chicken war," the U.S. Government has not made its stand on this violation. The U.S. position would, from the start, have been an irrefutable one. (See also the "War of the Chicken," p. 48 ff.)

* Data taken from the article "Der Poulet-Krieg," in the *Neue Zürcher Zeitung*, foreign ed., No. 221, Blatt 9, of August 13, 1963, updated to October.

pared with 5.65 cents for third countries—or a preference of almost 50 per cent.*

Within the framework of the EEC's regulatory policy, the relatively greatest freedom of price formation is envisioned for *fruits and vegetables*—products of great perishability whose markets are, in any case, largely governed by consumer buying power and demand. Accordingly, the EEC's policy with respect to these commodities is confined to the progressive introduction of common standards of quality to eliminate unsatisfactory products, meet consumer requirements better, and improve producer returns; and to provisions safeguarding against imports from third countries at abnormally low prices by temporary suspension of imports or a countervailing charge raising prices at entry to the level of "reference prices" to be established.†

In the case of threatened market disturbance, such safeguarding measures are also permitted in trade with other member countries. Market intervention is also envisioned.

Normal import protection for fruits and vegetables is by fixed tariffs only; these are being progressively abolished in trade between member countries, as in the case of other commodities and in accordance with the principle of gradual establishment of the customs union.

* In addition, in the case of poultry, as has been indicated, some member countries' offer prices are reduced greatly below those from third countries as a result of government export subsidies.

† It is to be assumed that such reference prices will be set, and are being set, at levels that in fact reflect the kind of crisis or emergency against which special protection can legitimately be sought. According to an authoritative statement by one of the Commissioners, third countries were officially assured that such reference prices will be set at so low a level that, should heavy imports take place and threaten serious market disturbance, the EEC will be upheld in invoking Article XIX of GATT to justify the import surcharges through which the reference prices would be implemented.

Regulations for beef, dairy products, sugar, and rice are still being finalized. Cotton—which, as a largely imported industrial raw material, is duty-free—is not an object of EEC's agricultural policy. Leaf tobacco is a fixed-tariff item;* however, the Commission is under a mandate to develop something akin to a "common agricultural policy" for tobacco, which might bring direct producer subsidies with or without production control, or perhaps worse provisions from the point of view of third-country exports.

To sum up the main content of the EEC's agricultural market and price policy, we might say that the most rigid protection is planned for the basic (so-called target-price) commodities. Others will be more flexibly protected. Grains, sugar, and dairy products are the basic commodities for which target prices are to be approximated systematically by variable import levies and/or export subsidies. (Products processed from these basic commodities fall under similar regulation and protection.)

Pork, eggs, and poultry will be protected by fixed tariffs and "derived" variable levies, the latter to correspond, theoretically, to the variable levy on imported grain feed by which the costs of domestic feeders exceed those in the exporting countries.† Fruits and vegetables will be mainly protected by fixed tariffs and market interventions.

For products other than the basic ones (for which target prices are to be enforced in any case), minimum import or

* Bound in GATT at 28 per cent ad valorem, with a specific minimum of 13.2 and maximum of 17.2 cents per lb.

† As mentioned above, such calculations (for imports from third countries) are based on prices of feed grains in the "world" market, as if the exporting third-country producer, everywhere, were able to buy his feed grains at such world prices. This is by no means the case. I am not aware that this point has been made an element in third-country representations.

gate prices may be decreed and realized by special levies.*

For oilseeds, it is not unlikely that a system of manufacturing taxes (margarine) will be imposed to regulate interproduct competition affecting highly protected animal fats. Without that, such competition might prove unmanageable under the established (zero) tariff for oilseeds and moderate fixed tariffs for vegetable oils.

* Theoretically, the establishment of a fixed gate price is for the purpose of protection against dumping or special disruptions of markets. Again, it is strange that U.S. interventions with the EEC regarding gate prices have not seized upon the fact that the EEC has confirmed that purpose by promulgating gate prices invariably with some such formula as "to avoid market disruption due to outside offers at abnormal prices." (Articles 7, 6, 6, and 11 of EEC Regulations 20, 21, 22, and 23 of January 14 [April 4], 1962, for pork, eggs, poultry, and fruits and vegetables, respectively.) As pointed out above, these regulations were before the Contracting Parties of GATT in the final 1962 negotiations. In some cases, the principle has hitherto been adhered to (for example, fruits); in others, the provisions have degenerated into additional protection or preferences for the commodity concerned (for example, poultry).

6. The Association of Overseas Countries and Territories

FOLLOWING THE expiration at the end of 1962 of the first Convention of Association between the EEC and overseas countries in Africa and dependent territories having special relationships with EEC members, a new Convention was signed in July, 1963, for the five years ending in 1967.

Association of these countries and territories is based upon Article 132 of the Treaty of Rome. Under it, their trade benefits from the same conditions the EEC member countries grant each other. Also, all EEC member states are obligated to provide the associated countries and territories with investment aid. Conversely, the latter are obligated to apply to their trade with all EEC member countries, and with each other, the same conditions they apply to the EEC states with which they have or have had special relations.

These general rules mean that the EEC member states progressively remove all import duties and abolish all quantitative restrictions on imports from the associated states and territories, as they do on imports from each other. Community preference on certain tropical products is to be speeded up. Also, the associated countries and territories are to get special consideration in the case of trade in products included, or to be included, in the Common Agricultural Policy of the Six.

Conversely, the associated states open their markets to the Six; but they may take, or retain, special measures to protect their economic growth in general and their infant industries in particular. Also, they will not join the EEC in a common tariff toward the outside world, so that their association is somewhat in terms of a free-trade area, with attendant problems of control and certification of the origin of goods exported from the associated countries to the EEC.

The preferences that associated countries or territories previously enjoyed in the markets of the EEC states with which they had special relationships will, under the new Convention, be measurably reduced.* Also, guarantees on prices and quantities previously extended to dependent territories by the metropolitan country concerned will not be maintained, since the EEC members will eliminate all quantitative regulation of their trade with each other and the associated areas.

But there are advantages that more than offset these drawbacks: the remaining preferences will be granted by *all* EEC member states; and special financial aid will also be given.

This financial aid to the eighteen associated African states is to total $730 million for the 1963–67 five-year period,† of which $620 million are to be grants, and the remainder loans. A total of $500 million is to be disbursed for investment and technical assistance. The remaining $230 million will be devoted to special programs of diver-

* These preferences will be smaller, because in the case of some products the EEC tariffs will be lower than the former national tariffs in the member countries where the associated states used to enjoy a preference. Also, the original common external tariff of the EEC will later be reduced by substantial margins for coffee, cocoa beans, tea (to be abolished altogether), pineapples, coconuts, and some spices.

† Associated *dependent* territories will receive grants of $60 million and loans of $10 million. Of the total EEC-country contributions, about 34 per cent each are to be borne by France and Germany, 14 per cent by Italy, and 18 by Benelux.

sification and other aid programs, which are to enable the countries to market their exports without the benefit of the special prices they used to receive.*

The Convention is renewable in five years; any member may withdraw from it on six months' notice. Association is open to all countries "whose economic structure and production are comparable to those of the associated states."† A Declaration of Intent, made by the EEC in April, 1963, in pursuance of an understanding reached between it and the United Kingdom during the 1962 negotiations, provides specifically that African countries of the British Commonwealth may seek some form of association with the EEC, either by joining the existing Convention or by joining under a separate association agreement of more limited scope.‡

Special Association Agreements have been concluded between the EEC and Turkey as well as Greece. Both agreements envisage a full economic union, to be attained in stages. While the EEC will begin to grant its concessions immediately and in rapid progression, Greece and Turkey will be permitted long transition periods, ranging from twelve to twenty-two years, depending upon the commodities concerned. The EEC will also provide special financial aid.

The special treatment the EEC countries extend, or will extend, to overseas countries in Africa and dependent territories, as well as to other less developed countries that

* The above as per FAO Conference Document C 63/10 of September 12, 1963, on *Regional Economic Integration* (Prepared for the Twelfth Session of the Conference, November 16, 1963), and *Information Memo* P-23/63 of July, 1963, by the EEC.

† EEC *Information Memo* P-23/63, July, 1963, p. 18.

‡ The potentialities of these provisions should be carefully weighed by third countries whose interests might be strongly affected. See also p. 44 ff. below.

have or will become associated, will no doubt bring to these areas economic and social benefits not shared by non-associated countries. This, of course, is clearly intended, and not only as a compensation for benefits that those areas, in part, enjoyed previously through their special relations to a metropolitan country in the EEC group.

A further trade-diverting influence is brought to bear by the fact that the customs union or benefits here concern countries of totally different structures and product composition of their output. In such a case, there is little pressure toward more economical resource utilization as reflected in trade creation within the union area and without, interregional as well as international. The more complementary, economically, the "joining" areas are, the less the economic gain from union; the more alike or competitive they are, the greater that gain.

It should be noted that the preferences and benefits to the associated countries are partly in terms other than tariff preferences; an important share of their exports to the EEC are materials that are not dutiable in any case. The commodities that might be affected by trade diversion as a result of the association policy of the EEC include coffee, cocoa beans, vegetable oils and materials, tropical wood, sugar, cotton, and tobacco. These effects are likely to grow, as economic development in the exporting or potential exporting areas proceeds and as other countries join in an association with the EEC.

Some of the international arrangements later to be suggested for agricultural trade may also turn out to be suitable for dealing with the problems raised for some non-associated areas by the EEC's association policy.

7. Seminar on Trade Policy

IN THIS chapter I propose to give, implicitly, some examples of how necessary it is for us, and for all prospective negotiators, to give more thought to the intricate matters of trade policy and of trade negotiations. We must develop a more imaginative approach; we must have a basic concept of what we are after, for everyone to see; and we must let our people gain sufficient experience and leave them in pursuits in which they can and must use it.

We must also strive for compatibility between what we do ourselves with what we demand of others. We must not say that variable import levies are incompatible with economic neighborliness while insisting that there is nothing wrong with variable export subsidies. We must not denounce as quantitative restrictions the variable import levies other countries impose to protect a domestic support program, when we, for the same purpose, impose direct quantitative control over imports. And we must not say that there is a difference because of our domestic supply controls, since these have in most cases been of questionable effectiveness. We, an economic giant with the highest standard of living, must see the problem of "access" to agricultural markets abroad in perspective when we negotiate voluntary limitations of exports to the United States by some of the poorest communities capable of exporting at all.

I still think that the United States and other countries have a right, even an obligation, to advocate and urge economic common sense in international economic relations, and hence in the economic and trade policies of partner countries. But our stand must be made with the earnestness of reason and humility that becomes each one of us when we contemplate our own imperfections as well as those of our neighbors.

The examples, with implicit lesson, as I said, will be drawn from the recent history of international-trade-policy discussions and actions. The exercise gives me a welcome opportunity to include, as a first point, some comments on the program for the 1964 GATT negotiations, the so-called Kennedy Round.

The Program for the Kennedy Round

In their GATT meeting in 1963, the Ministers decided mainly on the application of three principles for the Kennedy Round of negotiations:

1. Reciprocal, equal, linear cuts in tariffs for large groups of commodities, with special procedures (but generalized or automatic ones) to be adopted in cases of "significant" disparities in tariff levels among the participating countries.

2. Inclusion, by special treatment, of agriculture in the give and take of the Kennedy Round.

3. Efforts to reduce barriers to exports of less developed countries, without reciprocity.

At the same time, a Trade Negotiations Committee was set up to elaborate a negotiating plan and, within a short time, to agree on how to handle the proposed linear tariff reductions, how deep they should be, how tariff disparities should be determined and dealt with, and what acceptable rules for agricultural trade could be devised. It would have taken demigods to agree on even a fraction of this bill by August 1 (the deadline originally set); and, in fact, at the

time of this writing (December, 1963) *none* of these points
has been settled.

Among the reflections that suggest themselves on the tariff problem is the thought that our original hard line on
uniform linear cuts all the way through, regardless of
levels of present tariffs in the U.S. and the EEC, was not a
promising position. It will surely be necessary for countries with extremely high tariffs on some commodities to
agree to arrangements for adjustments that are *not* equal
on both sides. They will also need to make such a conces-
sion in order to gain acceptance for exemption from the
linear procedure of certain items, perhaps exemption from
any kind of tariff cut in some cases. The United States, too,
will have to come up with such cases.

Also, we must be under no illusion about the limited
value to the U.S. of the definition that we obtained of
what is a "significant" tariff disparity: that it must be
understood as "meaningful in terms of trade." There may
be isolated cases in which it could be shown that a steep
tariff increase did not reduce trade; and in such cases the
high tariff's disparity from what the other side has on that
item or group of items might be considered as not being
"meaningful in terms of trade." (Even then, the existence
of a *ceteris paribus* condition would have to be shown.) In
most cases, however, there will be no history of trade that
would permit a comparison between the effects upon trade
of a relatively low and a high tariff for a given item; and
it will always be an open question whether, if tariffs *had*
been much lower, trade might or might not have been
considerably higher. If one of the two parties were to assert
one of these conclusions, while the other denies it, there
would be no factual basis for proving the one right and the
other wrong. Thus we will still have to rely on reasonable
give and take in realistic compromises devising some sort of

mechanical formulas for the definition of what would be a *"significant* disparity." It is important to realize this for an appropriate posture in the negotiations.

There are other ramifications of the vague agreements made on "linear cuts," "equal cuts," and tariff "dispari-ties." I am not aware, for example, that, when told that the United States tariff had more high positions over 30 per cent than the EEC, we asked the EEC to what extent the calculations included their levies and tariffs and "gate-price" premiums on grains and livestock products of up to 110 per cent(!). These unheard-of rates apply to highly essential products and affect a substantial proportion of the EEC's trade; they could perhaps even be *shown* as being "meaningful in terms of trade."

The EEC's first answer would of course be that it has long been understood that it is precisely these "common-agricultural-policy" items that must be dealt with in sepa-rate arrangements on agricultural trade; and that they cannot therefore be considered in both segments of the forthcoming negotiations. There is some pertinence to this argument; yet it would be quite legitimate for the United States to include this pointer in our reactions, if only to reinforce the claim to a really worthwhile accommodation in the agricultural segment of the negotiations.

Another point about which very little has been said is that of the inclusion of countries other than the U.S. and the EEC in the Kennedy Round in GATT. And yet, a clear-cut position in this respect is of great importance. The GATT's basic rule is the most-favored-nation rule. All benefits we negotiate are automatically extended to all GATT countries. If it comes to the 50 per cent cut or somewhere near that figure on large groups of commodi-ties as provided for by the U.S. Trade Expansion Act, and the EEC and the U.S. join in an agreement of this kind, how about the other GATT countries? Of course, we are sure that the United Kingdom, as a leader of the West, will be fully prepared, and eager, to make equivalent concessions in order to earn ours and EEC's. But what about all the other GATT countries? What about Japan, Canada, Australia, Britain's EFTA partners in Europe, and some of the less developed countries that are on the way up and can afford to trade more liberally?

I do not mean to imply that these countries will just sit by as onlookers, expecting to get all the benefits of the Kennedy Round for nothing. National pride, diplomatic prestige, and what has after all developed over the years as an international code of honor will work to prevent the spread of such an attitude. And some of the countries particularly interested in lowering EEC barriers to reduce their preferential effect have already indicated their readiness for worthwhile participation. Nevertheless, it will most certainly be impossible to make them all bow to whatever "linearity," "equality of cut," or "disparity" the EEC and the United States (and Britain) would be willing to agree upon. They will have their own ideas about what is equivalent on their part and what they can afford.

This point is likely to prove a serious matter, not only in itself, but also because it might become the vehicle for an ultimate denial of reciprocity, as we see it, also on the part of the EEC and even Britain. It is quite conceivable that the EEC could, perhaps even rightfully, say to us: "We are perfectly prepared to join you in making these cuts in all these groups of commodities, provided the other GATT countries A through F do likewise. But they are not prepared to do so; hence, we can match your cut by a much smaller one only." This might be just a welcome excuse, or it might not be. In any case, there is a great problem there about which our preparatory public discussion has been silent.

Yet the outcome of the whole exercise may hinge on this point. It may require a new look at the most-favored-nation principle—a prospect we should dread to contemplate. In view of the legislative history of the Act, it may require a radical change in our government's interpretation of its authority under the Trade Expansion Act, possibly one to be newly agreed upon with Congressional leaders. A thorough study of this problem is essential for all participants in the Trade Negotiations Committee; governments must weigh their essential interests and authorities and those of their partners in advance, so that the committee can make positive progress toward the Kennedy Round and avoid an early deadlock.

In our preparations for what commodities to offer for large reciprocal tariff cuts, we must also be careful to avoid a stereotyped attitude, such as that "get the tariffs down" would in all cases appear as the ultimate wisdom of trade policy. Each commodity's case requires analytical scrutiny. An example for what I have in mind is given, for an agricultural commodity (tobacco), in the following section.

The Case of Leaf Tobacco

The case of tobacco affords a good example of the need for continuous review and analysis for the purpose of developing and adapting concrete positions on individual commodities. The temptation must be great to let things ride in a grand sweep on the assumption that "getting the tariffs down" suffices as the *ultima ratio* for the Kennedy Round. Nothing, however, could be more deadly for those negotiations than such an attitude; it could even jeopardize adequate and intelligent preparedness by the United States.

There are a number of considerations in the case of tobacco that bear a resemblance to those applicable to other commodities, among them the overriding importance of a decision as to which commodities or commodity groups the United States should include in its own initiative for wholesale linear reductions, and on which it should let the EEC or other governments take the initiative; on which it should be willing to accede to EEC's or other countries' linear proposals, and which it should insist, on its part, to exempt.

Furthermore, there is the important question of including or excluding commodities subject to quantitative restrictions or similar invalidations of tariffs either in the U.S. or in the EEC and elsewhere, and those which directly compete with, or substitute for, such commodities. (The latter case should have interesting applications. Take butter, for example: With quantitative restrictions on imports into the United States, we might hardly dare suggest to include that commodity in the sweeping wholesale cutting procedure; if we do not, would it make any sense to include margarine, although we have no quantitative restrictions in this case? There is an ominous silence in the public discussion on questions of this kind.)

After a hard battle in Geneva in the long and exhausting sessions of 1961–62, the United States finally got both an acceptable EEC tobacco tariff and specific minimum-maximum spread. It would, of course, always be a good thing to have further reductions. This, however, is *not* the main issue for the United States at the present time. The main issue is, rather, *to keep tobacco in the EEC a fixed-tariff item and to deal with discrimination.* The whole U.S. position should be geared to this overriding goal.

It is by no means certain that we will be able to keep tobacco a fixed-tariff item. The EEC Commission is under a mandate to draw up proposals for a Common Agricultural Policy on tobacco. Depending upon what kind of policy will be proposed and adopted, it may be one in which tariffs would still have significance, or it may be one that would invalidate tariffs.

In either case, the EEC should be unwilling to negotiate on the leaf-tobacco tariff. In the first case, they would not wish to give up budget receipts, since they will have additional budget outlays, for example, for financing producer payments. In the second case, they would not want to negotiate about tariffs knowing that their Common Agricultural Policy on tobacco would invalidate any tariff concessions. And, in this case, it would be stupid on our part even to want a tariff negotiation on tobacco that could only impose one-sided sacrifices upon the United States.

In the light of these considerations, a U.S. position to press for inclusion of leaf tobacco in the up to 50 per cent reduction procedure in the Kennedy Round would reflect unawareness of important ramifications. If the EEC takes the initiative and wants tobacco tariffs in that general reduction procedure, well and good; we would go along. In fact, we could consider such an EEC initiative as an indication that they will *not* invalidate tariffs by a Common Agricultural Policy. But the United States should not itself take this initiative and press the EEC for reductions, because this might bring on the very Common Agricultural Policy we do *not* want.

A number of further considerations support this position:

1. If the EEC wants to exclude leaf tobacco from the generalized tariff reduction and we agree, it will give us a

plus in our favor, at least psychologically: *They* have proposed, *we* have accepted.

2. A substantial reduction in our own tariff might have a considerable unfavorable impact upon segments of our own industry.

3. Those in the EEC who oppose a damaging type of Common Agricultural Policy have claimed justification for their opposition largely on the basis that the present tariff sufficiently protects EEC growers. If tariffs were to be substantially reduced, even these present opponents might be driven into conceding that a Common Agricultural Policy might become necessary.

No one should, of course, take lightly the objections that might be raised against such a U.S. position. But hard analytical work must be done to hammer out a final U.S. policy on this commodity. It must take into account the view that it is not the absolute level of the EEC leaf-tobacco tariff that is our problem. (It hardly could be, considering also the high fiscal charges and retail pricing of tobacco products.) The real problem is *discrimination* and the possibility of discrimination of various types.

While this issue of discrimination in actual fact centers around the association with the EEC of less developed countries, official attention has strangely emphasized *ad valorem* versus *specific* tariffs as an issue of discrimination.

First, as to a further narrowing of the spread between the specific minimum and the specific maximum of the EEC common tariff, this subject should, of course, be tackled. However, it lies outside the Kennedy Round's concept of linearity and equality or reciprocity. It should be separately negotiated in compensation for other credits that accrue, or have accrued, to us; but obviously it could not be fitted into the over-all process of "matching concessions."

Second, we should also note in this context that, although any narrowing of that spread is in our favor because of our higher prices and qualities, its existence cannot in fairness be termed "discrimination." Since the United States' basic tariff philosophy is *ad valorem,* we cannot complain that the system implies higher *absolute* rates on higher-priced products than on lower-priced ones (which, indeed, is the essence of the *ad valorem* system). In fact, one might, with greater justification, say that the previous *specific* tariff, for example in Germany, discriminated *in our favor,* since it implied higher *ad valorem* or percentage-of-value rates on the lower-priced tobaccos of other countries. To plead for specific rates on tobacco, in place of *ad valorem* rates, on grounds of discrimination is thus an untenable position that only could do harm and must be avoided.

The "War of the Chicken"

It is quite possible that the much-publicized dispute between the United States, the EEC governments, and the EEC Commission regarding chickens will have been settled, one way or the other, by the time this book appears in print. And in a number of public forays in the early part of 1963 (and in other ways even earlier), I have suggested a line of approach believed to be promising in the sense that it should appear fair and reasonable to both sides.* For various reasons it will be useful, however, to discuss the case here briefly to illustrate certain requirements for this type of negotiation, and to help toward a settlement in case no final one has yet been reached.

The main issue for the United States, in this context, is

* See, for example, "The Skirmish Line," in *The Journal of Commerce* (New York), August 16, 1963, pp. 4 and 14.

its export to Germany. Following a one-time arrangement in 1958 under the so-called Public Law 480 for U.S. shipments in the amount of $1.2 million (whose proceeds were exclusively devoted to market development in Germany), regular exports began to move. In rapid succession, U.S. exports to the common market rose to a value of $13 million in 1959, $23 million in 1960, and $53 million in 1962. Nearly all of these shipments went to Germany.

The German Government, up until the middle of 1961, still controlled chicken imports by quantitative restrictions. There was, at that time, a fixed import duty by value of 15 per cent. However, the quantitative control on imports operated to raise total protection to an incidence of about 30 per cent, as apparent in a comparison of import prices (free German border) and prices in Germany both for imported and comparable German birds.*

For reasons of general trade policy and under continued skillful pressure by the U.S. Government, the German Government abolished quantitative restrictions on chicken imports as of June, 1961. As a result, market prices in Germany were brought down, since the price effect of the former quantitative restrictions (as distinct from the effect of the import duty) ceased to operate, and consumption was thus further stimulated. However, in order not to reduce the degree of protection granted to German chicken producers, the Government, as of the day of the removal of the quantitative restrictions, granted a direct producer subsidy of equivalent amount (roughly 15 per cent). The subsidy was, at first, to be limited to small- and medium-sized establishments, but was soon extended to all.

Under this system, producer protection again amounted

---

* The protective effect of the quantitative restriction was also apparent from the price of freely traded import licenses (between 10 and 15 per cent).

to about 30 per cent (15 per cent import duty plus 15 per cent subsidy), and thus equaled the level that had existed under the system of quantitative restrictions. The new system continued until July 30, 1962, when the variable-levy scheme of the EEC (adopted on January 14, 1962) came into force.

Again, the German Government at first tried to keep producer protection unchanged. The total of the import charges—a fixed amount of tariff (11 per cent) plus a (variable) feed-cost differential of about 20 per cent—again was to give a total producer protection of about 30 per cent, the same as up to June, 1961, under the system of quantitative restrictions, and from June, 1961, to July 30, 1962, under the half price–half subsidy system. The subsidy was promptly abolished, by the German Government, as of July 30, 1962. What had changed, therefore, was not the *total* of producer protection, but the *form* in which it was granted. Since all of it is now in terms of price, whereas in 1961–62 a substantial part had been in terms of a subsidy, the present system is again more restrictive of consumption, as had been the pre-June, 1961, system.

It did not take much time, however, for pressure groups inside and outside Germany to see and seize their chance of actually increasing protection and production and of diverting trade from third countries to surplus producers inside the EEC. There were two devices that permitted such action: The first was the existence of a provision (in the EEC's poultry regulation of April 4, 1962) that permitted the establishment of "gate" or minimum import prices; the second was the fact that that regulation provided for such minimum import prices only toward so-called third countries, but not toward imports from other members of the EEC.

The EEC governments and Commission soon responded

to these pressures. Minimum import (gate) prices were
established, followed by up and down adjustments. By
stipulating that import prices cannot be below a certain
level, these gate prices are enforced by an additional variable import levy in the amount of the difference between
that "gate" price and the "offered" price. Thus, for example, if the import offer free German frontier for American birds is 30 cents per lb. and the minimum import price
is 33 cents, a special levy of 3 cents is imposed in addition
to the other import charges. The 3 cents, in this example,
would represent an additional charge of about 10 per
cent.*

With gate prices toward third countries thus adopted as
additional measures of protection for EEC producers,
France and Belgium seized the opportunity of abusing the
absence of a gate price on trading *between* members of the
EEC: the French and Belgian governments began to subsidize their chicken exports to Germany by as much as 30
per cent of the sales price.

U.S. reaction to the measures taken by the EEC on and
since July 30, 1962, was not as logical as it might have been.
It did not train its guns specifically upon the violations the
EEC was thus committing against GATT, against the
Rome Treaty, and against the basic theory of its own regu-

---

* It is obvious that such a system opens wide all doors to subterfuge
and fraud. The exporter who, with normal profit, could sell at 30 cents,
but actually offers and sells at 33 cents, can easily afford to dispense special "personal inducements" to importing firms; conversely, a fellow exporter's birds, offered at 30 cents, are taxed with an extra 3 cents of levy,
which goes into the coffers of the EEC. When the present writer suggested to an interested party the desirability of a fair and reasonable
arrangement that would assure, first, that the U.S. rather than the EEC
would cash in on that price differential and, second, that there would be
equitable participation among U.S. exporters in that price advantage, he
was given to understand that there was preference for the anarchy of
individual dealings with a system of personal inducements. For partisans
of private enterprise, this is a strange concept of competition, indeed!

The real issue on poultry in the EEC is, therefore, the EEC's violation of GATT's nondiscrimination provisions, and failure to comply with principles of the Rome Treaty and the basic theory of the EEC regulations themselves that were before the Contracting Parties in 1962, when they concluded the Article XXIV examination. Our *démarches* should have been based on this point of view, not, or not only, on our March, 1962, agreement with the EEC in GATT to continue negotiations after the effects of the variable-levy system and of our Trade Expansion Act are better known.

If this real issue has not thus far come to light in the public debate, it is because that debate has suffered from a lack of proper analysis. For example, even to this day some of our experts assert that the protection granted the German poultry farmer "has almost trebled," compared with the time before introduction of the variable levy on July 30, 1962. This statement implies that protection before July, 1962, amounted to 15 per cent, or the amount of the fixed tariff in force at that time. It thus ignores the fact that German producers, before July 30, 1962, enjoyed another 15 per cent protection through a producer subsidy, so that the total level of producer protection was actually twice as high. Finally, the statement ignores the fact that, with the introduction of the variable-levy system on July 30, 1962, the producer subsidy was abolished. Total protection, to be sure, is much too high, but it has by no means trebled;* we only weaken our case if we rest it on spurious arguments.

Of course, from the point of view of consumer prices and effects upon demand it is damaging that a producer

---

* The increase actually was from 30 to about 40 per cent, or one-third; and part of even that increase is due to higher feed costs and thus does not constitute protection of *poultry* producers.

subsidy has been replaced and overcompensated by import charges. However, do we want to advocate producer subsidies in place of tariffs or levies? And if so, have we ever mounted a campaign or an official *démarche* suggesting that the EEC adopt this principle generally, or in the case of poultry? The answer is: We have not. (Most probably we should have.)

In our negotiations for a settlement, we would have had a compelling case if we had based it on these contentions:

1. It is well understood that EEC regulations aim to provide a small preference for trade between the member countries before complete market unification brings with it the complete preference of a customs union. This principle of a small preference *cannot* now be unilaterally brushed aside by the subterfuge of establishing a gate price toward the "outside" but none toward the "inside"—and through this cunning device to make it possible for member countries (in the case of poultry, France and Belgium) to create practically any degree of preference for themselves by large government export subsidies.* Even after complete market unification, the preference for member country suppliers will be only 7 per cent (the amount of the common fixed-tariff element in total poultry protection), while the French and Belgian export subsidies raised that preference to as much as 30 per cent.

2. Consequently, all export subsidies between member

---

* The illegality of this device was implicitly confirmed in an official German Government statement saying that minimum import-price regulations for imports of poultry from member countries were not provided for in the EEC Market Ordinance of January 14, 1962, *only because it was assumed "that no member state could afford to make offers below the minimum import price for third countries since the latter is calculated on the basis of the lowest feed grain prices (world market) and the most efficient production."* (Erster Bericht über die Auswirkungen der EWG-Marktorganisationen fuer die Zeit Juli bis Dezember 1962. Gemaess Drucksache IV/725. Ministry of Agriculture, Bonn, 1963.)

countries must be ruled out; and if there must be a gate price, it must be the same toward member countries as toward third countries.

3. If there is to be a gate price, it must be placed at the level at which it would only represent antidumping protection fully in accord with Article XIX of GATT. The EEC could easily be held to compliance with that Article. For in countless references, its own Regulations have made it clear that the setting of gate prices would only be such as to prevent market disruption through dumping, and for that purpose only. These references were before the Contracting Parties when they negotiated about the compatibility of the EEC with GATT.*

4. Finally, since it is not unlikely that there is considerable padding in the calculation of the variable equivalent of excess feed costs,† the feed conversion formulas must be rigorously checked; any concealed protection thus discovered by objective analysis would compel its removal. Also, not world prices of feed grains, but prices that are actually known to rule in the third country, must be made the basis for calculating the feed-cost differentials.

An approach of this kind would still appear promising in that the EEC governments could not deny the relevance of our claims. It makes no sense to demand that total import protection for poultry be limited to a fixed percentage when we know that this protection includes variable elements (such as the feed-price differentials) calculated on the basis of objective criteria and linked in a logical system. We must deal with these individual elements without asking the EEC to tear the whole structure down, lest

---

* See also the assurances given by one of the Commissioners, referred to on p. 32, second footnote.

† Such padding may, for example, lie in assumptions of a grain share in poultry feeding far in excess of actual practice.

we give the impression of not having grasped the essence of the system.

Beyond that, the United States must show more concern about the German campaign against American poultry, a campaign that claims that American poultry is injurious to health and is said to have been a major factor in the decline of German consumption of U.S. poultry. If there is no substance to that claim, it should be possible to make drastic use of available international facilities and legal means in Germany to prosecute and silence this propaganda and to obtain resounding authoritative denial of the allegations. The U.S. Government might well spend some money on financing vigorous law suits by American exporters and German importers of U.S. poultry against the originators and disseminators of such stories.*

That the proposed approach is not altogether unrealistic has meanwhile been confirmed by very competent voices from Germany, the *Wirtschaftsblatt* of the *Frankfurter Allgemeine Zeitung,* the Ministry of Agriculture, and by the EEC Commission itself.

An article that appeared in the *Wirtschaftsblatt* on September 17, 1963,† calls for an "end to the chicken war" in very much the same terms as the present author had developed in the note in *The Journal of Commerce* (Au-

---

* This would be money usefully spent, more usefully than many a million that now goes for naught in trade-fair and public-relations efforts. A disquieting aspect of these efforts is the fact that no one really knows at which point they are to take effect: Are they aimed at the ultimate consumer, the retailer, the wholesaler, the importer, the government official who makes or administers rules and regulations, or at parliaments who make the laws that impede or facilitate trade, or perhaps at vested producer interests that dictate, in no small measure, to legislating parliaments? To ask this question means pointing at interrelations and influences that do not yield to the demands of palates or purses. Madison Avenue cannot modify the trade and agricultural policies of modern industrial society.

† "Schluss mit dem Hähnchen-Krieg," by Albert Seyler.

gust 16, 1963): to terminate the one-sided discrimination against third countries either by outright abolition of the gate price or by applying a reasonable gate price (at levels representing nothing more than an antidumping device) toward EEC member countries as well as toward third countries.

The German Ministry of Agriculture, in turn, continues to favor a revision of the EEC's "Poultry Market Ordinance" (No. 22) in the sense of abolishing the special discrimination against third countries by generalizing the gate price toward EEC member countries as well as third countries, thus holding to the position the German representative took in the EEC Council debate at Brussels on July 30, 1963.* At that time, Germany proposed that the "inside dumpers," so-to-speak (France and Belgium), on their part undertake not to sell below the minimum import price now in force only toward third countries. In September, 1963, the Ministry returned to this theme indicating (though not giving its overriding reason) that "it had always been Germany's endeavor to assure, for third countries, reasonable access to the Common Market." In this sense, it was contended, the EEC's "Poultry Market Ordinance" should be changed (meaning: the gate price should be generalized).†

Incidentally, here again, judging by U.S. criticism of the German role in the Council debate of July 30, 1963,

* This German position does not, of course, represent all insight and compromise in the broader national interest. It is very much a position that favors the German poultry producer above all. For the proposed action would terminate the damaging dumping on the German market of French and Belgian government-subsidized exports that, despite the apparent increase in protection, have held the German market under pressure so that the German producer's returns are now less than they were one, two, and three years ago.

† *Wirtschaftsblatt* of the *Frankfurter Allgemeine Zeitung*, September 17, 1963, p. 17, col. 4. Cf. also footnote, p. 55 above, with the interesting official German reference to the ominous omission in the EEC decisions of January 14, 1962.

it is obvious that U.S. observers did not grasp the meaning of what was going on: They did not understand that there should have been the greatest pressure of support for the suggestion of the German representative. Its acceptance would have eliminated many of the reasons for the decline of the U.S. share in Germany's poultry imports: the setting by the EEC of a gate price toward "outside" countries only, and exploitation of its absence toward "inside" countries by government export subsidies on the part of France and Belgium. The same lack of comprehension had previously made the United States refuse German overtures to press for the application of a minimum import price to imports from *all* sources.*

As far as implicit confirmation of this point of view by the EEC Commission itself is concerned, it is useful to note the Report that the Commission submitted to the Council on November 12, 1963, concerning developments under the variable-levy regulations during the first year of operation.† In it, the Commission pleads for a rescission of all export subsidies (so-called third-country restitutions) in intra-EEC trade and considers that setting minimum import prices at too high a level *would increase intra-area preferences to an extent not envisaged by the EEC regulations.*

On December 4, 1963, the U.S. Government announced retaliatory suspension of existing tariff concessions on a number of products, effective January 7, 1964. This, we

---

* This is just as important a point as is a sizable reduction in the absolute amount of the minimum import price, which the Germans have thus far opposed. And if we play our cards well, we might even get the Germans to agree to such a reduction and thus put the "inside dumpers" under irresistible pressure for accepting the (reduced) gate price for their own exports as well. For this is as much in Germany's true interest as it is in ours.

† Cf. *Europa—Land- und Ernährungswirtschaft* (VWD, Frankfurt/Main), No. 242-63, November 13, 1963.

should hope, will *not* end the chicken case. Since official comments on the announcement put the emphasis on *suspension* that could at any time be withdrawn,* all the more pertinent approaches indicated above should still be open to the United States. They would have a good chance to correct the situation and benefit the very product that has been disadvantaged, whereas retaliation benefits no one and only tends to poison the atmosphere between partners who are soon to launch and lead a world-wide exercise of trade liberalization. In fact, the announcement of retaliatory suspension of certain concessions has set the stage for a sensible settlement of the type we have discussed.†

Variable Levies and Gate Prices

A telling example of the lack of comprehension with which some American observers view the logic of the EEC's mechanics of protection is afforded by the confusion

---

* As per official announcement of December 4, 1963, and *The New York Times* of December 5.

† We cannot of course be sure that this opportunity will actually be pursued. Some of our more skeptical observers even contend that the U.S. authorities are so sick of the chicken issue that they desire "to sweep it quickly under the rug"—a purpose allegedly sought by prompt retaliation. These observers believe to find support for this contention in the fact that the announced retaliatory withdrawals will not really hurt the imports that have been selected. Thus, for example, the tariff increase for brandy will only affect a high-priced product for which price elasticity of demand in the United States is low or zero. Should there be more restrictive effects on the importation of trucks, these would paradoxically fall upon a country that is not the principal culprit in the case and which, had there been a clearer conception of the issue, could have been given effective support in fighting the U.S. battle inside the EEC. (Cf. the statements by Mr. Lahr and Mr. Hüttebräuker in the EEC Council meeting of October 14 and 15, 1963, referred to on p. 101, footnote.)

I do not share these suspicions. We will soon see whether or not they were justified. But it is obvious that the appropriate course will be much less comfortable for our negotiators than a tired resignation to consider the case as closed.

that exists with respect to the above subjects.

To most, variable levies are simply variable levies, and nothing else. And I have often been appalled to hear some who ought to know better ask why it is that there are gate prices (and gate-price-enforcing special levies that vary) for commodities other than the "basic" ones but none for the latter.

The answer is, simply, that basic commodities have specific target prices maintained by "threshold" prices which, in turn, are enforced by variable levies. In a sense, threshold prices *are* gate prices; therefore, in the system applied to those commodities, a separate gate price would make no sense.

It is such lack of comprehension of essential points in the EEC's system that complicates the U.S. position in negotiations with the EEC. Thus, too, on livestock products, exporting countries must not be trapped into misreading the protection levels sought or established by importing countries. France and Germany, for example, have long been known for their inordinate protection of grain and other crops, while livestock products were treated less generously. This sort of practice was largely terminated by the advent of the Common Market. In it, equivalence is to be sought between the protection for crops and that for livestock products; and most of the applicable regulations issued thus far serve this aim (which, as such, is only logical).

In the light of this conception we must see the variable levies component of the protection for livestock products (compensating for feed-cost differentials) in the EEC as *derived* ones, not as *primary* levies like those on grains. It follows that we cannot attack, or negotiate about, derived levies on livestock products as such; rather, we must address ourselves to the *grain* levies (or prices); and any adjustment we achieve will then automatically carry with it an equivalent adjustment for the livestock products concerned. *This is a point our policies have thus far largely failed to acknowledge.*

However, it also follows from these circumstances that we can and should attack and negotiate about the *conversion ratios* applied to the grain-feed component of livestock products from which the *derived* levies result. The *supplementary levies* that are due to the enforcement of *gate prices* are still another matter.

To emphasize once more the existing differences in concept and interrelationships, I offer the following summary:

Target-Price Commodities. For commodities for which a predetermined, specified price level is to be set and maintained in the EEC, this goal is sought by the establishment of a threshold price for imports at point of importation. This "threshold" price, in turn, determines and secures a specified "target" price in wholesale markets and, through it, producer prices at corresponding parities. The mechanics of this protection is the *imposition of variable import levies—the levies always being the difference between the predetermined threshold price and the lowest c.i.f. import price corresponding to EEC "quality parity."* (The system works only in cases where there is a considerable net import requirement; parallel mechanics, in the case of commodities on an export basis, are variable export subsidies.)

This pure system of the variable levy at present applies exclusively to grains. It fully covers any needed differential between any given c.i.f. import price and the desired domestic price. *In such a system, there is no room for any additional levy such as, for example, a gate-price provision would imply.*

Market-Price Commodities. Commodities for which there is no definite price aim or price guarantee are not protected by variable levies, or at least not by variable levies of the pure type. They are basically protected by fixed tariffs, or temporarily by quantitative restrictions, or both. If the basic protection of such a commodity also includes a variable levy, this is not a variable levy of the pure type *but simply the variable equivalent of the variable protection granted to an element in its cost of production.* (Livestock products such as poultry, eggs, and pork are examples; their "variable levy" is to be only the equivalent of the variable levy on the cost-element "grains," and therefore a derived, not a primary, one.)

Industries producing commodities in this market-price category—*commodities that have no guaranteed or target prices*—thus have *basic* protection by *fixed* import charges only (although total protection may include a variable compensation for variable import charges on cost elements). However, since such *fixed* import protection does not provide any safeguard against extraordinary declines in world market prices, the EEC regulations provide (for some of these industries) a special additional protection—a specified minimum import price or gate price—against such declines.

Such a minimum import price or gate price can, of course, only be enforced by the imposition of a special levy that would at all times raise import prices to the specified minimum or gate level. If world prices for such a commodity vary and the gate price is to remain unchanged, the levy that enforces the gate price must, of course, also be a variable one.

In theory, the establishment of a fixed gate price (also called minimum import price or reference price), enforced by a variable import fee, is for the purpose of protection against dumping or special disruptions of world markets. This purpose is confirmed by the rules thus far formalized: Gate prices (also called minimum import prices or reference prices), in fact, have been invariably promulgated with some such formula as "to avoid market disruptions due to outside offers at abnormal prices." (Articles 7, 6, 6, and 11 of the Regulations Nos. 20, 21, 22, and 23 respectively, of January 14, 1962 [April 4, 1962] for pork, eggs, poultry, and fruits and vegetables.) The theory has thus far been adhered to in the case of fruits, but was badly violated in the case of poultry, where it degenerated into additional (and quite illegal) protection.

It is essential that third-country governments be at all times aware of the philosophy the EEC itself has expressed for the gate-price concept. It was before the GATT parties in the negotiations of 1960–62, and was one of the bases on which the EEC's system of agricultural protection was condoned; and it is regrettable that the EEC was not held to it in the famous case of the chicken war.*

* See also the assurances given in 1962 by one of the EEC Commissioners with respect to "reference prices," as mentioned in the second footnote on p. 32 above.

8. Toward an International Policy on Agriculture

WE SHOULD, by now, have assembled a sufficient number of relevant facts and considerations to pause for a moment of reflection. Is there any prospect at all of finding a way out of the dilemmas posed by the national interests, politics, and policies of individual countries? Can there be a negotiated accommodation between the need for agricultural support and the need for maintaining international trade in agricultural products?

I do not believe that anyone could, with candor, claim to be sure of the answer. If I have in the past made suggestions for broad outlines of a settlement, it was not in the belief that my suggestions would prove the most acceptable and workable. Rather they were made under the influence of two circumstances: first, the belief that the dispute over agricultural trade poses a real threat to international economic and hence political relations and that it was therefore worthwhile, even necessary, to seek solutions to the problem; second, the impression that there are elements in the situation that might permit an approach of reason and compromise and hence, in my opinion, an approach not perhaps likely to succeed, but the most likely to succeed.

Beyond that, I have been impressed by the need for further work on the facts, on background and analyses, and on efforts to comprehend and truly understand the various principles and systems of agricultural protection and trade policy. And this need for further work, from which realistic positions might result, has appeared compelling in light of the present stalemate in our international debate: three and one-half years have elapsed since the EEC Commission presented the essential logic of its agricultural market and price policy; and two years have elapsed since the members of GATT have given in to the unyielding insistence by the EEC countries on this policy. Yet, instead of meeting the opponent on its own firmly claimed ground, EEC's partners still find it advisable to press for the very negation of that logic by demanding fixed tariffs or equivalent fixed import charges. There is still confusion as to original variable levies and derived ones. And the real chances of holding the EEC to clearly undertaken commitments and provisions of their own rules are still being missed by unrealistic attempts to recover a position that we were unable, or unwilling, to hold two years ago.

It will perhaps seem understandable that, in such a situation, workers in the field are sorely tempted to carry on and advance their own ideas on what appear to them realistic ways to handle the problem.

The U.S. Government and other governments have not, of course, been idle in the three and one-half years that have elapsed since the nature of the EEC's forthcoming policy became fully known through the Commission's agricultural proposals of June, 1960. However, no comprehensive plans have been advanced and debated. The only specific attempt at a proposal, in general terms, was the Pisani Plan (on which, however, details were cautiously withheld); and the only international debate of points for an agreement was in the EEC–U.K. negotiations to which no other countries were partners and which were necessarily confined to the immediate issue of British accession to the EEC.

Aside from recent proposals by the EEC Commission—

submitted to the EEC Council in November, 1963—international explorations and discussions thus have been confined to generalities. Where there were references to concrete proposals, they were often marked by insufficient realism. To the exclusion of any other arrangements, suggestions seemed at times to center on the expectation that the EEC would readily give worthwhile quantitative import guarantees for a number of important products. For a variety of reasons, we should not be too confident of satisfactory results in this respect.

At other times, exporting countries seemed inclined to say that if producer prices in the EEC were to be set at reasonable levels—say, half-way between the high German and the lower French prices—their interests would appear taken care of, and in that case, they would not need to ask for any other commitments. Nothing could be further from realism. We know next to nothing about the responses of supply to price for the various agricultural products in the various circumstances of individual countries. Moreover, there is a high probability that, for reasons pointed out previously, price unification in the EEC at any conceivable level will have a built-in tendency toward expansion of output.

Some suggestions also expressed the hope that the EEC could be induced to lower drastically the variable import levies now in effect; and it is still seriously believed that for some products, so-called tariff quotas (quotas at low or zero tariff) and specific limits to variable levies could be negotiated. The fundamental principle of the EEC's agricultural policy is the maintenance and full protection of yet to be determined producer-price levels for basic products. These, in turn, determine automatically the height of the import levies and require their variability. Hence, those hoped-for measures would be altogether incompatible with the fundamentals of EEC policy.

In the negotiations on agricultural trade in GATT's Trade Negotiations Committee and in the separate Commodity Groups we must leave all this behind us. We must show an understanding of the realities of the situation and aim at balance between the desirable and the possible, both as to essence and as to form. And we must not give the impression of having failed to grasp the basic principles of the EEC's agricultural policy. It will be the better part of wisdom for outside countries first to tackle their EEC problems at the soft spots, so-to-speak; and to seek accommodation in manners that would not require the surrender of fundamental positions. In time, perhaps, as international understanding grows, they too will become subject to modification. This possibility is more likely to materialize if we do not now insist on choosing the most difficult approaches.

Our negotiations must be wholly subservient to the thought that they are to prepare for an international policy on agriculture and agricultural trade—in other words, to prepare for a world-wide approach to a special code for agriculture within the framework of GATT.* A concrete content for such arrangements must be derived from facts

* It is perhaps worthwhile to record here what, in any event, would appear to be a strong moral commitment of the EEC to contribute helpfully to the kind of compromise solution that is needed as between requirements of national agricultural support and the equally important goal of trade maintenance. During his visit to the United States in April, 1963, EEC Vice President Mansholt urged that the forthcoming negotiations deal not only with barriers to trade as such, but also with "decisive elements in all our farm policies" that are the real crux of the trade problems. Only then will it be possible to find that compromise between the interests of "our farmers at home" and "the legitimate trading interests of other nations": the development of "a code of good behavior in agricultural policy." (*European Community,* April–May, 1963, No. 62, Washington, D.C., and *Foreign Agriculture,* April 22, 1963.)

and considerations of the type presented in this review. They will best be built on the basis of a general philosophy and some broad principles that follow from it. This sequence will also prove to be the most effective approach for tackling the actual negotiation of such agreements: first to discuss and agree on general principles, and subsequently to negotiate the details of implementation.

If there have been no comprehensive plans and debates thus far of an international policy for agriculture, there have certainly been worthwhile thoughts and suggestions on segments of this great problem. In developing realistic elements of an international policy, it will be useful—and not only for reasons of strategy—to consider and carefully weigh these contributions. Governments, organizations, and individuals who have wrestled with the problem must be given the satisfaction of seeing their thinking and planning recognized in all those respects that would appear to help a realistic understanding. If each contributor were to insist on his own ideas to the exclusion of those from any other source, we would not get very far in writing an international policy acceptable to all.*

---

* Among the contributions made to the quest for a realistic policy on agriculture and trade, I would like to mention, again, the French plan that has become known as the Pisani Plan, first advanced two years ago, featuring special arrangements on international and internal prices, on demand supplementation and, to some extent, supply management. Then there are the many policy resolutions and policy studies contributed by the International Federation of Agricultural Producers (IFAP) and its secretarial staff, with proposals on commodity agreements with price regulation, demand supplementation, supply management, and trade arrangements, and strong emphasis on the need for adequate support of such international arrangements by national agricultural policies. There is also a plan advanced by the British National Farmer's Union embodying proposals for supply control at home (and elsewhere) and quantitative trade arrangements in commodity agreements. There are the OECD (OEEC) studies and resolutions on agricultural policies since 1955; studies made in the FAO and in the EEC/FAO Agriculture Division in Geneva; statements of the problem by the Executive Secretary of the GATT; and the Guiding Principles for national agricultural price stabilization and support policies

Before I present, in consolidated and up-dated form, another attempt at giving our efforts a further push toward the desired goal of a realistic program for agriculture, I shall review in detail the two proposals that will, in any case, occupy strategic positions in the negotiations: The Pisani Plan of November, 1961, and the EEC Commission's proposals of November, 1963, on grain price unification and on the negotiations on agriculture in GATT. It is particularly fitting that we should have a closer look at these two plans when we contemplate a compromise between the interests of major importing and exporting countries; for it is the EEC's policy that agricultural exporters primarily fear, and within EEC it is France's aspiration for agricultural gains that offers the greatest problems.

We should also carefully note specific contents of the EEC–United Kingdom negotiations, whose status as of January 29, 1963, was described in a report by the EEC Commission issued in response to a resolution of the European Parliament. The report deals with the situation as

---

recommended by an FAO study group and accepted by member governments in 1961. Furthermore, there are proposals endorsed by working groups of the Atlantic Institute in *Atlantic Partnership* by P. Uri (1963), to the effect that developing countries should, in place of direct food aid, receive money earmarked for imports of food; and the important proposals by J. Royer made under the auspices of the International Chamber of Commerce on effective undertakings for the maintenance of agricultural trade. A prominent place must, of course, be given to the propositions on price and production policies, minimum and maximum quantities for world trade, stocking policies and trade with the developing countries to be treated in world-wide agreements according to the understandings that had already been reached between the EEC and the United Kingdom toward the end of the Brussels negotiations in August, 1962. Finally, there are the British Government's specific suggestions for agricultural trade and corollary changes in its own agricultural and import policy of October, 1963; and, as mentioned above, the EEC Commission's proposals on immediate unification of grain prices and for the GATT negotiations on agriculture, of November, 1963.

it had developed up to the time when the talks were suspended.*

In emphasizing that the British problem of Commonwealth trade could only be solved in a wider framework, the six EEC countries themselves started from the premise that a solution must be sought through world-wide arrangements. In the tenth session of ministers (August 1–August 5, 1962), it was agreed that the Community, including Britain, would take the necessary steps toward calling an international conference to negotiate principles of arrangements for grain, meat, dairy products, and sugar. The conference was to find a reasonable compromise between the interests of importing and exporting countries, and to assure rational development of international agricultural trade. It was also agreed that the conference would negotiate price and production policies, and trade with the developing countries. Minimum and maximum quantities for international trade and stockpiling policy were to be examined also. These commodity agreements would be revised at three-year intervals, and special institutions would supervise and control their execution.

Time and again the Report asserts that the European Economic Community realized that it had a great international responsibility in regard to agriculture and trade and that it was fully aware of the implications of this responsibility. Full agreement could not, of course, be reached in the negotiations during the first days of August, 1962, because, with respect to some products, the EEC had not as yet decided upon the type of internal policy it would apply. This, however, in no way detracts from the commitments made with regard to the principles that were to

* *Bericht an das Europäische Parlament über den Stand der Verhandlungen mit dem Vereinigten Königreich.* Brussels, February 26, 1963, EEC Commission.

serve as a reasonable compromise between agricultural protection and international trade in agricultural products.*

The basic question, then, even from the EEC's point of view, can no longer be acceptance of certain principles, but rather the methods that might be applied to carry them out. Since the fundamental purpose is to continue income support for agricultural producers in most importing countries and some exporting countries in a manner applying economic common sense and still allowing a reasonable volume and value of international trade to move with equity, it follows that there will have to be some undertakings that would limit the growth of production in relation to requirements, and measures to facilitate the expansion or supplementation of demand, commercial as well as noncommercial.

* See especially Chapter II G of the *Bericht*.

9. The Pisani Plan*

IN NOVEMBER, 1961, the French Minister of Agriculture, M. Pisani, and the then French Minister of Finance, M. Baumgartner, in FAO and GATT, respectively, presented the outlines of a plan for agriculture and trade in agricultural products. Since its subject is agricultural trade, and since it has become almost the official position of one of the Common Market partners, its importance to international economic policies is obvious.

The Plan is an outgrowth of the problem that the proposed agricultural policy of the European Common Market presents for the "outside" countries, and of the desire on the part of the French authorities to find a formula that will help outside exporting countries to become reconciled to the gains French agriculture hopes to make in the markets of the EEC.

The Plan

The partial expositions of the Plan thus far published start with a critique of what is called the present organization of world markets in agricultural products.† This

* This chapter appeared originally in the *International Journal of Agrarian Affairs*, III, No. 5 (June, 1963), and is here reproduced, with some adaptations and extensions, by courtesy of the *Journal's* Editor.

† For an outline of the Plan, see Michel Woimant, "L'Organisation du Marché Mondial," in *L'Agriculture Française, La Nef*, Nouvelle série, Cahier no. 11, July–September, 1962. Also M. Pisani's communication to the Council of Ministers of the EEC, at Brussels, June 29, 1962 (reproduced in *Informations et Documentations Agricoles*, No. 13, July 15, 1962). I also understand that there exists an outline circulated in April, 1962, in the seminar of M. Van Ruymbeke at the École Nationale d'Administration giving a description and explanation of the Plan.

critique contends that no developed country can afford to abandon its agriculture to the prices ruling in the so-called world market. Some important commodities are internally subsidized or price-supported everywhere and divorced from export pricing; in the conditions of a mixed farm economy, one might add, this gives support to agriculture as a whole. Hence, the concept of a world price has lost all meaning. In present circumstances, no one could say what world prices should be on any rational basis; their present levels can only be interpreted as the balance of counter-vailing influences and historical continuity.

It is ridiculous, exponents of the Plan point out, that France, for example, should subsidize its industrial competitor Britain through deliveries of butter at half its cost. It is equally ridiculous that the United States should furnish Germany grain at low prices only to complain later that Germany's currency reserves have grown at the expense of the U.S. balance of payments. And it is the height of folly for Western exporters to engage in a price war in order to furnish, at the lowest price, the cereals needed by Communist China. Competition among a number of important exporters has generally made for "world prices" below the costs of production that would allow for reasonable incomes for families on well-managed farms.

On the other hand, none of the developed countries now buying so cheaply in the world market would expect its own producers to supply consumers at such ruinous prices. And where they do not support farm prices directly, they let consumers pay through taxation for farm subsidies. They have, therefore, little reason to object to higher import prices.

The exponents of the Plan further contend that the developed countries have not sufficiently explored the possibilities that exist for equilibrating supply and demand.

Liberalist policies, such as have been suggested for agriculture and industry, are socially and politically impossible. International commodity agreements of the traditional type have proved incapable of dealing with the problem of surpluses. And there has been inadequate exploration of the possibilities for developing outlets for food in the poor countries that cannot now afford to pay for additional imports.

If efforts at surplus disposal for economic development in those poor areas remain confined, in the main, to one large donor country, there is the danger of encroachment upon commercial transactions. If other donor countries come into this trade, there is the danger of "food-aid competition" and an oversupply even for aid purposes: food aid must be given in terms of what is traditional or can be made acceptable in the needy areas; it may even be that surplus output will have to be converted into different commodity compositions; and this can only be done by an efficient, joint *international* effort in which several countries participate. Also, there must be firm assurances, within firm agreements, that recipients of food aid can count on a long-term supply that will not be withdrawn at short notice.

The Pisani Plan takes its cue from this critique of the present agricultural-trade situation. The most important elements of the Plan can best be summarized under two headings: (1) prices; (2) demand and supply adjustment.

1. Prices. The essence of the proposed price policy is an upward adjustment of world prices for commercial trade that would eliminate all export subsidies. The international price would be raised to the level of import parity for the producer prices in the most important consuming region—the European Economic Community.

Such an action, to be taken in an international agreement, say, on grains, would also serve to hold prices within the EEC more readily to reasonable levels. This point is made quite clearly in the expositions of the Pisani Plan, but usually overlooked by critics of the price proposals. Other commercial importing countries would aim at identical price goals, so that only *one* international price would rule all commercial ("solvent") markets. And just as export subsidies would disappear, there would be no scope for import levies in the importing areas.

The arrangement would give exporting countries higher sales proceeds, even at lower quantities of trade; the excess receipts would be available to finance programs of surplus giveaway to needy nations. It makes no sense for exporters to sell at lower prices if any difference is to be skimmed off, by importing countries, through variable levies—as is now the case in the EEC.

2. *Demand and supply adjustments.* The proposals recognize that, at the new prices, world-market equilibrium might well be threatened unless something is done with respect to supply management and, especially, on the demand side to create new outlets for surpluses.

With respect to supply management, the proposals envisage a special arrangement with those exporting countries like Canada, Australia, and Argentina who either pass their export proceeds back to their producers or might be inclined to do so even when international prices are raised. The Plan foresees that these countries, in return for the advantage of higher export prices, would commit themselves not to pass on to their producers any price increase that might induce an increase in production (export taxes). This, too, is a point that critics of the price proposals usually overlook.

For other exporting countries, such as the United States,

with relatively high support prices, the Pisani Plan would foresee a continuation, or tightening, of supply control, as well as a price commitment. It is not clear to what extent the Plan contemplates supply control in importing areas, including the EEC (with France as part of it), other than what might result from the setting of reasonable producer-price levels.

So far as demand adjustment is concerned, the Plan simply postulates that any remaining or inevitable excess of supply over commercial demand should be used for a massive concerted international program of food aid. It believes requirements for food aid to be almost limitless, provided a determined effort is made to educate consumers in those countries to eat more of the West's traditional foods, and provided also that the West is willing to produce the commodity composition wanted by noncommercial demand as diligently as it produces the composition wanted by commercial demand.

The Policy Intent

The French Plan has a number of ideas that must be considered good and practicable from any reasonable point of view. And it has a measure of logical elegance that gives the reader and critic the joy of addressing himself to suggestions that are intellectually provocative. There are other ideas in the Plan that, if properly modified or supplemented, might well serve as practicable provisions for an international compact. But there are still others that could neither bear rigorous analysis nor pass the test of reason in the context of international cooperation.

From the standpoint of France's national interest, the Plan is calculated to serve the purpose of gaining and expanding lucrative markets for French agricultural exports.

There can be no question about this foremost aim of the French initiative. The French Government has often asserted that its agreement to partnership in the EEC—with alleged French "sacrifices" on the industrial side—was predicated on agricultural arrangements favorable to French agriculture.

Higher international prices would benefit France's agricultural exports to countries outside the EEC where they now bring only the world price. This is an important aspect of the Plan, and non-EEC markets have, at least until recently, taken a very large share of French agricultural exports.

Furthermore, implicit in the price-raising proposals of the French Plan is the suggestion that countries turn their attention from the *quantity* of trade to the *value* of trade as the real thing that matters. And there is a strong implication to the effect that it would be more realistic for outside exporters to seek maintenance of the value of their shipments to the EEC rather than maintenance of quantity —which, in any case, would be out of the question.

Again, this would serve an eminently national interest of France, since it would keep open the possibility of commercial disposal within the EEC of stepped-up French output. France would have access to the EEC for larger quantities and values of exports; outside exporters would perhaps realize as much value for their exports as before. France would thus gain, and outside exporters might avoid losses; but the importing areas (both inside and outside EEC) would have to foot the bill in terms of higher import prices.

While there are these favorable aspects of a world-price adjustment so far as France is concerned, the Plan also asserts that it would benefit outside exporters by providing them with additional means (through higher prices) from which to finance the giveaway of surpluses that cannot be disposed of through commercial channels. Whether or not there would be this effect would seem to depend entirely on how much in total value of exports—at higher prices for smaller quantities—those countries would gain. If they just managed to *maintain* their export value, nothing would be left to finance the giveaway; it would have to be financed as heretofore. And, in any case, if there were such an increment in value, it would again come out of the pockets of the commercial importing countries inside and outside the EEC.

It should be noted, however, that underdeveloped countries, as beneficiaries of food aid, would stand to gain under the French Plan—provided they could use effectively more surplus foodstuffs than they are now getting. For, from the French Plan's operation, more surpluses would result for food-aid transactions; and longer-term commitments and possibly adjustments to a better composition of food-aid availabilities might open up additional aid outlets.

Some Comments

There can be little quarrel with the Plan's thesis that present world prices of important agricultural products have no rational basis and that there is nothing sacrosanct about them. But when it comes to justifying the proposal that world-price levels be set at the standard of "the most important commercial importing region," the Plan's economics becomes flimsy indeed.

"The classical theory of the markets indicates that the price should establish itself at the level of the production costs of the marginal producer, in other words, at the cost level of the production that is the least profitable, yet indispensable fully to satisfy commercial demand. . . . This marginal producer is, for all practical purposes, the producer in the principal commercial importing region, the European Economic Community, enlarged by Great Britain."*

This argument breaks down upon consideration of the fact that the supplies of producers with lower production costs go begging for noncommercial disposal only because government policies prevented them from filling commercial demand reserved for marginal producers in "the most important commercial importing region." The argument also evaporates when its authors suggest that the higher world prices should not be passed on to producers in low-price exporting countries in order to prevent an increase in production there—an increase that, presumably, would to some extent determine which price and which country or producer in which region is the marginal one.

I do not believe that the good sense of the proposal of higher international prices can be helped by such reasoning. The question is not one of economics, but one of economic policy, and I am satisfied that there is a lot to be said in favor of such a policy. But before a final judgment can be reached, there must be a thorough international debate from a number of points of view.

First of all, the question of raising the international price within the framework of a commodity agreement (supposing that such an agreement can actually be brought about) would be a matter of serious concern to those commercial importers outside the EEC such as Japan and a few other countries that have hitherto been able to import at relatively low prices. The whole question is not just one of logic, but also one of historical continuity—a principle that is of greater practical importance than the French Plan appears to contemplate.

* Michel Woimant, *op. cit.*, p. 122 (author's translation).

Furthermore, the Plan makes no reference to the problem of how to handle, say, the transition of trade from
giveaway to commercial trade in certain underdeveloped
countries; or how to handle the coexistence of giveaway
imports with commercial imports in an underdeveloped
country. This latter case is by no means unrealistic; it is
precisely such coexistence that has led to the so-called
normal-marketings concept in U.S. surplus-disposal operations.

Another problem is the international pricing of commodities other than grains. Any agreement on grain prices
that would raise international prices significantly might
have far-reaching effects upon price formation for other
agricultural products, especially livestock products, both
in domestic trade and in export trade. It might completely
change present relationships in international competition.
This is another point at which the factor of historical continuity comes into the picture as one of the problems that
must be considered both with respect to competition and
with respect to possibly restrictive effects upon demand.

There are other aspects that should be weighed. Among
them are the possible analogies that other countries may
draw for the export pricing in international trade of their
own products. If the rich countries, as it were, by deliberate action improve their terms of trade for exports of
grains, why should poor countries exporting, say, coffee
not be entitled to a similar arrangement? It is true, of
course, that in the case of grains, being food or readily
convertible into food, measurable additions to normal
commercial demand could be and, to some extent, are
being brought about by special food-aid programs—a supplementation of commercial demand that could not be
said to be possible in the case of coffee. This very consideration points up one of the weak aspects of the French Plan,

namely, the lack of clear-cut recognition not only of the
need for supplementation of *demand*, but also of the need
for effective *supply* management in both exporting and importing areas.

No economist will disagree with the French Plan's contention that there is no particular virtue in any of the
present international grain-price levels, nor in any of the
national price levels; and that, if prices are being managed
or otherwise set or guided by a multitude of policy judg-
ments and influences, they will rarely be such as to per-
form properly their normal function of equalizing supply
and demand. Hence, something needs to be done to substitute for this function.

The French Plan primarily concentrates on additions to
demand through food-aid programs for less developed
countries. Even those sympathetic to the idea must urge
the utmost care to avoid overestimating the "effective"
potential for surplus disposal. To deal with the supply side
as well is a *sine qua non* for realistic policies.

Again, thorough international debate of these issues is
essential for a mature judgment of the Plan. The French
idea of supplementation of demand through food aid might
well be linked to effective supply control. For example, as
I shall explain below, it might be possible to bind all exporting and importing countries in an international agreement to place into stocks, either for holding or for surplus
disposal, agreed amounts that would represent the best
possible estimate of the quantities that cannot be disposed
of commercially of the export supplies available at present
levels of production. Moreover, there might be an arrangement to the effect that any increment over and above
present production, or production in an agreed reference
period, should be so neutralized.

The amounts that should serve as a base, so to speak, for
each country would, of course, be the result of negotiation,

and it should be possible to make allowance for justified increases here and reductions there, in accordance with the basic idea of reasonable arrangements. However, the general plan would still be one of linking the implementation of food aid with supply control. And there would be other possibilities for effective supply management, either directly by producers or by governments.

In taking a position in international negotiations, France may well wish to start out with a claim for exemption from supply control. But it cannot expect that other countries will necessarily agree to so one-sided a proposition. There will, in the end, have to be a compromise. The French Plan is not too clear on this point. The French hinted that the United States and France have been the only countries practicing effective supply control—the United States by its well-known restrictions and France by limiting its price support to a specified "quantum" (of wheat, for example). If this were the type of supply control envisaged for France, its acceptability from the international point of view would depend upon the quantitative price and output relationships contemplated under it; and it would also depend on how it would fit the *general* system to be negotiated.*

With respect to internal producer prices in importing areas like the EEC, the French Plan, as indicated, contemplates import parity with international prices at or near present French levels. Realistic approaches will be needed to explore additional possibilities, both as to the international level and with respect to producer prices in importing countries. International scrutiny of the Pisani Plan cannot shy away from a discussion of the problems it raises, whether they are expressly stated or only implied.

---

* Supply control in the United States has always been of questionable scope and effectiveness, and the French quantum system under EEC is on its way out.

The Commission proposes that EEC Community funds be utilized to compensate the governments of Germany, Italy, and Luxembourg for the direct payments they make to their farmers under this plan: fully, during the first three years of its operation; and on a declining scale beginning in 1967 (two-thirds in 1969).

In connection with these proposals for immediate unification of grain prices, the Commission also urged the Council to adopt, for implementation beginning in 1966, so-called Community Plans for the Improvement of the Standard of Living of the Agricultural Population. While these suggestions have found little public and foreign government resonance, they deserve attention. For it is quite obvious that they represent another attempt by the Commission to press for Council rules and decisions concerning measures for structural improvements.*

The Community Plans are to include financial support, by the individual governments and the EEC as such, for regional development schemes that aim to improve agricultural as well as general economic structures in less developed EEC regions; special programs for problem farmers in problem areas (mountain farms, dwarf farms, remote locations, etc.); and measures for the improvement of social programs in agriculture.

In its concluding remarks, the Commission once more alludes to the possibility of more general income payments in supplementation of measures of this kind and, one might add, of price policy. It looks as if the idea of a mixed support-price–producer-payments system is gaining ground, although it seems hard for the Commission to discard altogether its original objections.

---

* Cf. p. 23 ff. above. The Commission's tenacity with respect to this important part of the CAP deserves our admiration.

An evaluation of the grain proposals of November, 1963, can be brief. The acceptance of the idea to make immediate price unification possible through direct producer payments is commendable. The linking of such payments to important aims of productivity improvement and social policy is likewise most reasonable; and one cannot help being impressed by the astuteness with which the Commission, in its proposals on financing, has tried to bolster these aims.

On the other hand, the grain-price levels envisioned would seem to be too high; the present French wheat basis should have been regarded as the maximum, once direct income payments were proposed as a compensatory measure, and out of Community funds at that. It must be admitted, however, that the Commission was in a most difficult position with regard to the price level, and had to avoid overplaying its hand. For no matter how desirable a more rigorous suggestion may have been, the pertinence of Germany's emphasis on "real" rather than "nominal" prices cannot be denied altogether.*

The financing of the income payments with each country's own funds rather than Community funds would constitute a desirable pressure for moderation of producer protection. But here again, the Commission had to see to it that its proposals command some appeal precisely in the countries that will be hit by the price reductions. Also, its "Community" ideology must, of course, look askance at a perpetuation of separate country policies in the face of the long-desired CAP.

A regrettable feature of the grain-price proposals is the

* There is also, I am informed, a suggestion that the temporary income payments made to German farmers should in part be financed out of the increase of producers' prices in France. Thus, as the payments to the Germans would decline gradually, the returns to the French would increase gradually. There is a meritorious thought in this idea as well.

absence of any ties of the producer payments to supply
control, other than indirect and longer-run effects that
may emanate from the payments devoted to productivity
improvement and social support. Admittedly, again, it
would not have been easy for the Commission to provide
for such control, notably in a framework which maintains
that the producer payments would be "neutral" as to individual products. Yet, the desirability of such links could
have been acknowledged and left for further exploration,
were it not for a much more disquieting attitude that Mr.
Mansholt is reported to have shown in the Council discussion of his proposal. According to that report he is said to
have remarked: "The market organization, as it results
from the agricultural regulations already adopted, evi-
dently implies the disappearance of the *quantum* notion.
If the government of France has maintained such a *quantum,* it has been in contradiction of the established rules."*

On the whole, I think the Commission's attempt at price
unification is laudable, despite the less desirable aspects
that have been pointed out. It is the Commission's implicit
attitude and the claims it makes for the proposal rather
than the proposal itself that offer grounds for concern. I
have already touched upon supply control. Furthermore,
it is only too obvious from the comments with which the
grain-price plan is submitted that the Commission expects
an agreement on price policies to be the main objective
and, indeed, requirement of the GATT negotiations on
agriculture.† Price policy, the Commission contends, is
production policy. And, beyond that, it emphasizes its

---

* *Le Monde,* November 7, 1963, p. 15, col. 3. (Author's translation.)

† This assumption is confirmed by the "Second Mansholt Plan"—the
Commission's proposals of October 30, 1963, regarding the negotiations on
agriculture in the GATT round also presented to the EEC Council on
November 5. (See *Le Monde,* November 7, 1963, p. 5.) The plan is discussed in the following chapter.

belief that the target levels for grains as now proposed will not lead to an objectionable expansion of grain output in the EEC and would leave present import requirements of about 10 million tons unchanged for the next ten to twelve years.

Chapter 12 records my profound distrust of price as the only regulator of demand and supply in the circumstances with which we deal in this review. At the same time, I have indicated my belief that we ought to favor a "configuration of prices" which would be a healthy one.* There is no reason why perseverant discussion and negotiation could not lead to arrangements which to maintain trade will rely partly on price, but not on price alone.

* See p. 108 and footnote.

11. The EEC Commission's Proposals for the GATT Negotiations on Agriculture

THE SECOND Mansholt Plan—as it was termed by *Le Monde* of November 7, 1963—is a communication of the EEC Commission, dated October 30, 1963, and presented to the Council on November 5, together with the proposals for grain-price unification. It outlines the Commission's ideas on how to negotiate, in GATT, on agriculture.

The communication diplomatically combines a liberal philosophy, which should appeal to EEC's partners in GATT but commits no one, with the proposal of actual commitments that would protect EEC's agriculture while giving little promise of protecting trade.

The philosophy is subtle and bewitching: it issues not only from the positions taken by the highest authorities of the EEC Community, but also from the Resolution unanimously agreed upon by the Ministerial Conference of GATT in May, 1963. Thus, the negotiations are to extend to *all* classes of products, industrial and nonindustrial, including agricultural and primary products. Acceptable conditions of access to world markets for agricultural products should be established so that a development and significant expansion of world trade can take place. And no element susceptible of affecting the equilibrium of the world markets for agricultural products should, *a priori,* be excluded from the negotiations—as the EEC Delegation, transmitting a declaration of the EEC Council, had specifically stated in the Ministerial Conference.

In emphasizing the need for expanding international trade in farm products, Mr. Mansholt's communication next draws a somewhat less bewitching conclusion: Given the well-known characteristics of the demand for food, such an expansion depends essentially upon an increase of shipments to areas where consumption is still low. The Ministerial Resolution of May, 1963, Mr. Mansholt implies, did not answer the fundamental question: How can an expansion in agricultural trade be reconciled with the equally important aim of protecting the standard of living of the agricultural population in the developed countries and of establishing a better economic and social balance in the developing countries?

The communication, descending further from the lofty generalities favoring expansion of trade to the rough and tumble of daily politics, next points out that certain exporting countries appeared to think that it was simply up to the importing countries to create acceptable conditions of access to their markets, while exporting countries themselves needed only to observe a certain discipline in the allocation and pace of their exports. Under such a concept, Mr. Mansholt contends, the importing countries alone would be burdened with the responsibility of reconciling the aspirations of national producers with the exigencies of foreign trade. This concept, he says, is unacceptable to the European Economic Community. The Commission would insist that *all* parties, exporting as well as importing, share in the obligations that should be established for the solution of the problem at hand—a commendable principle, but not perhaps scrupulously applied in subsequent suggestions for concrete arrangements.

In view of the manifold measures of protection practiced

in importing and exporting countries, trade negotiations on agriculture cannot negotiate on tariffs but must negotiate on the levels of *total agricultural support* in all countries. In the opinion of the Commission, it is possible to determine, for each product separately, the extent of the total support accorded by the various measures practiced. It is this total degree of support, product by product, which, the Commission proposes, should be negotiated and consolidated or bound in the forthcoming trade talks in GATT.

In addition to such consolidation, the Commission calls for the negotiation of world-wide agreements for those commodities that suffer from a "permanent disequilibrium" between supply and demand.

In its proposal of rules for the negotiations on agriculture, the Commission suggests that the total degree of protection for each product can be measured by the difference between the price of the product on the world market and the proceeds received by the national producers.* For any product exclusively protected by a fixed tariff, that tariff would measure the degree of support.

In the Commission's further definitions, the world-market price from which the degree of support is to be measured need not necessarily be the current world-

* The Commission expresses the view that the studies undertaken in various quarters, especially those made within the framework of GATT's Committee II, have already ascertained the most appropriate methods for measuring the total degree of support. Members of the Committee II study group, who have served in their personal professional capacity, are likely to disagree with this view. Aside from the more general problems that arise (set forth in Appendix: II. Measuring Degrees of Support or Protection), it would hardly be possible to allocate, product by product, general agricultural subsidies paid globally, not by product: subsidies for input items, per unit of plowland or acreage as such, per family, or the general social or productivity subsidies· *that are neutral as between products which are now being advocated more generally and which the Commission itself now proposes in its suggestions for immediate grain-price unification.* (See previous chapter.)

market price. Rather it should be what might be called an ideal or theoretical price called "reference price": The reference price would be equal to the current world-market price if the latter is considered reasonable and "representative"; if not, a reference price would be separately agreed upon. In any case, whether the world-market price to be used as a yardstick were to be the current price or a specifically agreed reference price, *it would be a fixed price:* hence, degrees of support would be bound *in reference to a fixed price;* consequently, too, where internal support would exclusively consist of a support price, the negotiated binding would, in fact, represent a binding of that domestic support price. Also, any variation of actual world prices up or down would be neutralized by corresponding inverse variations in variable import levies or export subsidies; the resultant "actual" reduction or increase in degrees of support would not be considered as such, since support is measured from a *fixed* world- or reference-price level.

Based on these methods and concepts, the Commission would envisage a binding of the amount or degree of support for each product concerned, as ascertained and interpreted in the manner that has been indicated. Countries would be free to negotiate levels of support to be bound lower than the levels at present in effect; the EEC, however, would, as a rule, not negotiate further reductions in its own support levels but would be willing to bind the present ones, although a negotiated reduction or increase in certain cases should not be altogether excluded.

It goes without saying that levels of support to be bound for each negotiating country and product would by no means be equal, but would differ, just as tariffs bound differ as between countries and products. Every three years a "confrontation" of agricultural policies would determine renegotiations or confirmations of the original bindings.

Countries should be authorized to make adjustments in their support levels for changes in the "value of money" (or general price levels) *during* any three-year period. If, in cases of emergency, a participating country feels forced to increase the negotiated level of support, it may act unilaterally, but must subsequently submit to a preagreed forum and procedure for the determination of compensations.

Finally, with regard to World Commodity Agreements, the Commission considers that, in accordance with the Ministerial Resolution in GATT, such Agreements should complete the general compact on agriculture. They should be concluded for products whose market balance has been (or is expected to be) basically upset and should have as their purpose the achievement of long-term equilibrium between supply and demand and of short-term stability, including an improvement and stabilization of world market prices. The Agreements should also result in a better food supply for less developed countries whose needs cannot at present be backed by international buying power; and it is probably in this context that the Commission envisages the restoration of long-term market equilibrium "mainly through an expansion of existing demand," while the achievement of short-term stability might be up to the envisaged stocking policies. International machinery for these purposes would be set up.

Within what the Commission calls one single *accord mondial* (world arrangement) of three-year duration, agreements are proposed for grains, some dairy products, sugar, and oil products. (It is not known whether meat was purposely omitted.) The GATT countries participating in the 1964 negotiations would all accede to the Agreements; other countries could also join.

The Agreements' provisions would include upward adjustments of world prices on the basis of reasonable returns for "the marginal quantities necessary to satisfy commercial demand [*la demande solvable*]." World-market equilibrium must not be sought by limitations on production as long as a potential noncommercial demand exists. An expansion of noncommercial demand in the less developed countries might later be sought by work on necessary infrastructures, transportation, port and storage facilities, other improvements in distribution, etc.

A terminal provision should also be noted. For the quantities "manifestly in excess of thus enlarged demand," the World Arrangement is to provide for methods of disposal and for rules aimed to prevent the production of additional surpluses. The undertakings to be given to this effect by exporting and importing countries are to envisage: (1) either certain agreed results, for the achievement of which the countries would undertake to carry out appropriate policies; (2) or obligations with respect to the use of certain instruments of agricultural and commercial policy; (3) a combination of (1) and (2).

It is not easy to come to grips with the Commission's proposals for negotiations on agriculture. They are, as I have already implied, a skillful mixture of common sense and diplomacy, of homage to liberal ideas and readiness for not so liberal practical action. Yet, they mean progress and include much that should help toward acceptable arrangements on agriculture.

With a bow in the direction of M. Pisani, the proposals include suggestions for the negotiation of higher world prices; suggestions for demand supplementation through an international giveaway program as the main equilibrator for supply and demand; and refusal of supply control until all noncommercial demand is met. The proposals do not contain any hint as to how supply is to be allocated as between commercial and noncommercial demand—that is to say, to what extent individual countries would share in the burden of demand supplementation through surplus disposal. Failing any principle of supply control, or on quotas for trade maintenance or for commercial output, the implication must be that importing countries would have the task of caring for the aspirations of their producers, while exporting countries would fill the world's giveaway pool.*

But there are bows in the direction of agricultural exporting countries as well. The proposals include, prominently, a scheme for binding the extent of "total agricultural support" in all participating countries, albeit at levels too high for satisfactory maintenance of trade. Yet, some sort of sympathetic gesture toward the idea of "no further increase in protection" has thus been made. At the same time, total reliance on binding degrees of support through commitments on prices appears to be suggested for the correction of market disequilibrium—an exclusivity that would scarcely appeal to exporters interested in effective maintenance of trade. Total reliance on binding degrees of protection measured from reference prices which —because they are *fixed*—cannot reflect the influence of even the smallest degree of competition or of changes in cost levels is not only excluded as a matter of practical politics, but also implies shaky, if elegant, economics: there is no logical analogy in binding "levels of protection" under a system of variable import levies (such as the EEC has) to the traditional binding of fixed tariffs under a system of variable prices.

* Which would be just about the opposite of what Mr. Mansholt accuses "certain exporters" of suggesting. See p. 91 above.

Since the Commission's proposal suggests "bindings" in GATT, it has the ring of a genuine alternative to what used to be a tariff binding. It does not seem, however, that this will bear rigorous scrutiny. Even if the "reference" prices were to be renegotiated from time to time with a view to preventing increases in the true "degree of protection," the commitment would not assure the maintenance of a reasonable volume and value of trade.

Finally, the much-heralded new type of commodity agreements—within a World Arrangement—would carry little content other than a setting of world prices and provision of world surplus pools for food aid to noncommercial importers. The mysterious reference, at the end of that part of the Commission's discussion, to undertakings by participating countries for agreed methods of "resorption" of surpluses *in excess of demand supplemented by all that food aid can bear,* and methods to prevent further such accumulations, are vague and noncommittal, sufficiently so to be susceptible of opposite interpretations. While this may or may not have been intended as the familiar method by which international conferences produce unanimous reports, it is in any case not very helpful in a situation in which all partners must fully respond to the call *hic Rhodos, hic salta.*

Specifically, with respect to some important points, observers will note that, despite the laudable acknowledgment of the need for internal policy adjustments to make the international compact work, there is a sweeping escape-clause provision: Even the very limited obligations undertaken by importers and exporters may be unilaterally abrogated if a party to the *accord,* "because of a given situation," feels constrained to cast them aside. (Subsequently, it would only have to submit to a procedure that would fix compensations to be accorded trade partners disadvantaged by its action; no provision is suggested for restoration of the *status quo,* once the "given situation" has passed.)

We will also note specifically that, on price agreements, the criterion is to be levels "satisfactory at once to exporting countries whose receipts are, or could become, insufficient" and "to importing countries desirous of guaranteeing the maintenance of a certain income to their farmers." This rule will be difficult to apply in practice, even if supplemented by the formula that such price levels are "calculated on the basis of the marginal production costs of the quantities still necessary to satisfy the commercial [*solvable,* effective] demand." This is the reasoning of the Pisani Plan as cited on p. 79 f. above: "The classical theory of the markets indicates that the price should establish itself at the level of the production costs of the marginal producer, in other words, at the cost level of the production that is the least profitable, yet indispensable fully to satisfy commercial demand. . . . This marginal producer is, for all practical purposes, the producer in the principal commercial importing region, the European Economic Community."* I hope to have dislodged this argument in the comments on the Pisani Plan: Supplies of producers with lower production costs go begging for noncommercial disposal only because they are prevented from filling commercial demand that government policies reserve for marginal producers "in the most important importing region."

* Michel Woimant, *op. cit.,* p. 122. (Author's translation.)

12. Points for a Compromise

REALISTIC SUGGESTIONS for an international accord on agricultural policy and trade must, of course, aim to strike a balance between opposite interests. This goal will most nearly be reached if we begin to develop our proposals from a basic philosophy that most parties can agree upon. Certain broad principles follow from that philosophy, and we may hope to find much, though not quite as much, agreement with them as well. In proceeding from the broad principles to the details of a concrete settlement our task becomes more complicated; the closer we come to measures of practical policy, the more difficult is it to find an acceptable mixture of arrangements that will in part satisfy one group of interests, in part another, and in part will just be found bearable by all. A settlement of this kind might well be called a realistic compromise.

The *general philosophy* that, in this exercise, we may take as acceptable to all would include the principle of international political and economic cooperation and, with that, an acknowledgment of the desirability of efficient resource utilization throughout the world; hence the need to maintain and expand international trade. At the same time, this philosophy acknowledges the importance of political realism and of graduality in needed adjustments that affect the physical and spiritual welfare of men—a graduality that has become a basic tenet of modern economic policy.

The *broad principles* that can be derived from the gen-

eral philosophy and from the attitudes already made
known (and on which we may thus hope to achieve a
measure of agreement) include the avoidance of further
increases in protection, and in impediments to consumption, except in dire emergencies; the acceptance of economic common sense as a guiding principle of considerable
importance despite its rejection as the *sole* determinant
of the pattern of world production and trade; the recognition of productivity increases as the basic need of
agriculture and its only true and undisputed source of income improvement; the recognition of the need for long-
run equilibration of supply and demand, with a positive
attitude toward the possibilities of deliberate management
of both sides of the equation; and the recognition of the
need for international agreements with definite commitments regarding national policies that will serve to accomplish these purposes.

In a discussion of detailed arrangements that would
implement the basic philosophy and the broad principles
mentioned, we should remember that any plan for negotiating a compromise between the interests of agricultural protection and of trade must be based on both a positive and a negative set of elements. The positive set would
include what hopeful ingredients we find in the principles
and practices countries now pursue; the negative set would
comprise the "sticky" points—those where strong political
commitments, superstitions and suspicions of vested interests, and deeply ingrained fears permit little elasticity.
I need not give here examples of what I have in mind; the
two types of elements will identify themselves in the course
of our discussion.

It is, of course, quite possible that the negotiations on agriculture will be so difficult, and hence so drawn out, that
developments in production and consumption in several

countries will in the meantime overtake the aims of the negotiation. In that case, agreement would prove still more difficult: It is easier to accept and hold to a *status quo* than to turn the clock back.

Furthermore, the problem of agriculture in the EEC and of agricultural trade is charged not only with domestic politics, but also with explosive foreign-policy issues. Attitudes toward an "independent" nuclear defense of Europe are tied up with it, and the problem itself has received such dogmatic treatment, especially in France, that, in my view, there is a real possibility that the European Economic Community will not in fact materialize, or that it might be so thoroughly modified that the remaining problems will have to be thought through anew.*

Yet, no matter how problematic all attempts at finding a workable solution to the dilemma of agricultural support and trade might be, we must continue our search.

The detailed arrangements to implement the principles that have been mentioned should, of course, be negotiated

---

* It is certainly not probable that the mighty machinery of integration, after having gathered momentum for almost five years, will suddenly grind to a halt. Too many levers have already been pushed and too much personnel is busy keeping the wheels going. Yet, the seriousness of the confrontation between mercantilistic and liberalistic influences within the EEC must not be underrated. One need only contemplate President de Gaulle's warning, in his press conference of July 29, 1963, that the Common Market might come apart unless its Common Agricultural Policy is cut and dried by the end of 1963; and Germany's reaction to the effect that, without a determination and steps toward eliminating the distortions of competition by subsidies and other support measures in member countries, and some decisions on policies safeguarding trade with third countries, the German Government will not be able to agree to new regulations for dairy products, beef, and rice and thus to approach completion of the Common Agricultural Policy. (See the reports on the meetings of the EEC Council of Ministers September 23–25, and October 14–15, 1963, especially statements by Under Secretary Hüttebräuker, of the German Ministry of Agriculture in both sessions, and Under Secretary Lahr of Germany's Foreign Office in the session of October 15, as per *Neue Zürcher Zeitung* of September 27, 1963, and a German Government *Informationserlass* of

as a component of the trade talks in GATT now set to begin in May, 1964. It is, after all, and despite existing opposition, in the framework and as part of this negotiation that arrangements on agricultural trade will have to be worked out.* They will need to include commodity arrangements with commitments on international and internal prices, subsidies, demand supplementation through international food aid, and supply management through import quotas, export quotas, commercial-output quotas for compliance by farmers or governments, and producer payments of a social character and/or tied to structural improvements with shifts or withdrawals of land or labor from agriculture or certain agricultural uses—some or all of these in loose coordination or systematic combination.†

October 16, 1963.) At the end of December, 1963, agreement was reported on the commodities mentioned. But the basic dispute remains unresolved.

* M. Pisani, France's Minister of Agriculture, has often proclaimed that the discussion on agricultural trade should *not* take place within GATT, but rather in an *ad hoc* conference on international agricultural commodity agreements. (See, for example, *Le Monde*, June 8, 1963.) There is of course no reason why the commodity committees that will discuss the possible agreements could not bring in interested non-GATT countries. Also, GATT members may well concede that such an *ad hoc* conference be called at an early stage to discuss some general principles, and possibly another one later to put the finishing touches on what must now be prepared in detail. But the negotiations as such should take place in the committees that have been set up by GATT; and the final agreements, also, must be firmly tied in with the 1964 GATT round for the further reduction of trade barriers, as has already been decided by the Ministerial Meeting of May 1963. Their nature as an essential component of the Kennedy Round must thus be preserved.

† These are the elements for negotiation and agreement which the present author has suggested in a number of previous proposals and which he summarizes here in up-dated form. Cf. the contributions published in the *Journal of Farm Economics*, August, 1961; *Kyklos*, XIV (1961), Fasc. 3; *The Times* (London) March 19, 1963; *Kyklos*, XVI (April, 1963), Fasc. 2; *The Commercial and Financial Chronicle*, March 7 and August 15, 1963; *International Journal of Agrarian Affairs* (Oxford), June, 1963; and in a paper presented to the Chatham House Conference on New Directions for World Trade held at Bellagio, Italy, in September, 1963.

Prices and Producer Payments

In the international arrangements toward which we move, agreements on prices will be of considerable importance. *International* prices will in any case be discussed; and for such products for which there will be commodity agreements of an older or newer type, minimum-maximum ranges will have to be negotiated in the interest of stability, even if a substantial concerted increase such as M. Pisani suggested were not to be carried out.

With respect to *internal* prices, a mixed price-support–producer-subsidy system might be sought, at least so far as the importing countries are concerned, and as a transitional measure. The proposal is linked to three ideas: (1) to make possible income support that assures a minimum standard of living, yet is neutral as between products produced; (2) to facilitate the realization of the principle that protection should not be further increased; and (3) to facilitate supply management and agricultural adjustment and promote productivity by trying to direct income payments (producer subsidies) to structural reform. These purposes show why a support system of this type is of interest not only to the countries where it might be applied, but also to their partners in trade. It is thus a legitimate subject for the trade talks and discussions of an agricultural code in GATT.

A variety of such systems is conceivable. They all could be neutral with respect to the choice of products produced; and they all could be so framed as to assure farmers "a minimum standard of living." Yet, there would be significant differences with respect to political and social ramifications as between, say, a system under which producer payments are calculated and paid straight per acre, and one under which these payments are given to small farms only and related to their farm acreage, or size of family, and the like.

An important example of a mixed price-support–producer-subsidy system is afforded by agricultural policy in Sweden. As a general proposition, that policy aims at a price level for agricultural products that would cover the costs (including reasonable incomes of farm operators and labor and a reasonable rate of interest on capital invested) of well-managed farms of from 25 to 50 acres of arable land.* This much support is granted via the price system.

In addition, in special consideration of the need for an active policy to improve the structure of agriculture and to recognize the more difficult situation of small farmers, a well-conceived program of agrarian reform and social support rounds out the market and price policy.

Small farmers get help and priority in the acquisition of farm land offered for sale; the government provides funds for the purchase and afforestation of unsuitable farm land, especially of older farmers with no children on the farm, and prevents its transfer to new ownership for agricultural use; and credits for improvements of land and buildings are restricted to farms that promise to become economically viable units. Social support to the small farmer, complementary to the market and price policy from which, because of his small market share, he benefits little, includes subsidy payments to each farm, based upon and graduated by size of farm acreage and/or deliveries of milk, the mainstay of the small farmer's cash income.†

---

* So-called basic farms (Agricultural Act of 1947). In 1959, the Government and the farm organizations agreed that from 1965, the cost calculations (and income comparisons with nonfarm workers) should be based on "norm farms"—well-managed farms of from 50 to 75 acres of arable land situated in the (more productive) plains.

† Subsidies per farm increase with increasing acreage up to 18 acres, then decrease to 25 acres, the "small-farm" limit. Similarly, the supplement

The Swedish system is, of course, not the only one in the mixed price-support–producer-subsidy category. Since price support is not entirely absent, the British system of deficiency payments is another example, although it does not aim at structural reform and social policy. Still another would be a system in which the income payments would be *directly* tied to the achievement of sound structural adjustments.

Something of this type is envisioned by the *Gemeinsames Gutachten* (Brussels, June, 1962) drawn up for the EEC by eight experts dealing with the possible effects of lower producer prices upon Germany's agricultural incomes, and—prior to the *Gutachten*—in the study by Professors Plate and Woermann in Special Issue No. 14 of *Agrarwirtschaft* (May, 1962). Aside from traditional assistance to structural reform through government aid in land consolidation, the building of farm roads, and the like, the authors emphasize the method of temporary, direct income support not tied to specific commodities. Such income payments could be capitalized, either for investment in the case of farms still capable of productive reorganization or, for compensation to the people affected, to facilitate transfer to nonfarm jobs and early retirement.

Some of the various features of these mixed support systems are also discernible in the programs of other countries. And the blueprint of the EEC's farm policy itself, in the concept of a well-managed farm as a yardstick, and in its ideas for structural adjustments, has from the start had ingredients of similar purpose and scope. Even the antagonists in the Common Agricultural Policy debate, French Minister of Agriculture Pisani and German Minister of Agriculture Schwarz, have more recently expressed

---

payments for milk deliveries decrease for quantities in excess of 26,000 lbs. per farm per year.

a positive attitude toward direct producer subsidies as well as price supports, albeit for divergent reasons.*

In view of these facts and considerations, it should not be altogether unrealistic to expect that governments, when they sit down to discuss agreements on policies for agriculture and agricultural trade, will explore the possibilities of mixed price-support–producer-subsidy systems much more thoroughly than they have in the past.

The EEC Commission, as indicated, has now made a proposal for such a system in its suggestions for immediate unification of the prices for grains. Although the price level proposed is on the high side, the acceptance of the idea as such and its suggested realization through producer payments marks great progress. Establishment and protection of internal prices could, in each country, be carried out through the EEC system of variable levies. The variable levies between EEC countries would disappear forthwith. *Market* prices would thus at once be unified, while *producer incomes* could be protected, through the device of income payments under the mixed system. That these payments could be directly tied to purposes of social policy and structural reform would, of course, be an advantage.†

---

* Cf. *Neue Zürcher Zeitung, Abendausgabe,* September 13, 1963, Blatt 3. While M. Pisani is not averse to subsidizing the producer (rather than the product) in such a way as to bring about structural reform, and with it the hope of a later cessation of the need for subsidies, Herr Schwarz expects permanent subsidies for the German grain producers to compensate for any possible income reduction resulting from EEC grain prices below the present German level. M. Pisani's attitude is, however, not quite so sweeping as his phrase: "Subsidies will no longer be granted to agricultural products, but to producers." (*Le Monde,* October 16, 1963, p. 20.)

† In the present author's proposal for such a system (*Journal of Farm Economics,* August, 1961; *Kyklos,* April, 1963), unified prices for grains were envisaged to be set at or below the 1960 French levels. It was thought that a practical determination of the size of the producer payments could be based on the annual calculations of farm income and living standards that have become a statutory obligation for the governments of the United Kingdom, Germany, France, Italy, and others. While the Commission

Whether or not income payments ultimately could be dispensed with altogether throughout the Community and producer prices truly unified would depend on developments that cannot now be foreseen. In fact, it would be one of the beauties of a mixed system that it would retain much of the approach the EEC has chosen yet would afford flexibility: to move gradually toward total integration in agriculture if that proves feasible, or retain a measure of differentiation if that proves necessary. The members of GATT should readily accept, as in their interest, such differentiation, even though it may not comport fully with the GATT requirement for completeness of a customs union. (Nor should the members of EEC be troubled by the postponement or suspension of complete unification of competitive conditions for agriculture within the area as a result of differential producer prices. For it is only too obvious that, in any case, unification of variable input costs and charges will have to wait for a very long time and may never be fully accomplished. One need only contemplate the many forms of direct and indirect support, subsidies, old age and other relief, social security, differences in taxes, freight charges, etc., to realize this.)

---

proposes that the payments be disbursed from Community funds, it had been my thought, as indicated above, that they should come from each country's own treasury, so that there be some pressure for restraint in protection. I even implied (*Kyklos,* April, 1963) that increases in agriculture's productivity should be paralleled by commensurate decreases in protection. I now wish to reverse this position. While the theoretical notion of measuring degrees of protection in relation to productivity is no doubt correct, the practical policy postulate to which I tied it now appears to me to be unrealistic. In all industrial countries, the desire to raise farm incomes more nearly to industrial income levels is strong, and this purpose is partly laid down in mandatory legislation. There could be no progress toward it if all productivity gains were neutralized by a decrease of protection. My original policy proposition will, however, become realistic wherever and whenever agricultural productivity has been substantially increased.

Matters of this kind will have to be discussed in the agricultural negotiations, whether price and subsidy measures were to be sought as substitutes or as supports for direct undertakings on trade, production, and surplus uses. I think the latter approach should prevail. Price management alone would not suffice to equilibrate supply and demand (even as supplemented by surplus disposal for aid); yet the "configuration of prices" certainly remains important in the context of equilibration.*

Producer Payments from Product Taxation

Gradually, as the discussions on price unification dragged on in the EEC, the Commission began to advocate temporary producer payments, and German and French Government and farm leaders have become reconciled to the idea of direct income payments to substitute in part for more favorable prices, as indicated. This gradual change in attitude culminated in the Commission's proposals for grain price unification of November, 1963. Most economists would agree with the Commission and M. Pisani that such payments should from the outset get a time limit and should be tied to structural adjustments or social aims, not to individual commodity output.

---

* I would not for a moment wish to imply that prices could or should be set without regard to rational aims including at least a trace of the supply-demand equation. When I contemplate some of the price problems in agriculture I like to reread, and re-enjoy, Sir Hubert Henderson's classic article on "The Price System" (*Economic Journal*, December, 1948), though he addressed himself to different issues. He who was "convinced that . . . direct, physical controls, working otherwise than through the price system, will remain indispensable in some important sections of our economy" still gave as the first proposition he wished to emphasize the dictum "that even when our economic activities are subject to a multitude of physical controls . . . the influence of the configuration of prices which exists at any time remains strong, far-reaching and fundamental. It is important, therefore, that this influence be a healthy one, that the configuration of prices should be such as to pull in directions which accord with the public interest."

The evolution in thinking, compared to the days when producer payments were scoffed at by the Commission, might offer a possibility of probing into still another scheme that would help the cause of reasonable international compromise. Whether before or after price unification, producer prices in the EEC countries for basic commodities (for which target levels are set) might be reduced by, say, 10 per cent. A turnover tax might then be imposed upon the first-line buyers of those basic farm products (wholesalers, processors, cooperatives) equivalent to the price reduction effected at the farm-gate level.* The yield of this tax would, in the end, be distributed to the farming community as income payments in a *global* fashion, based on farm acreage or some other general criteria, not on individual-commodity output or marketings.

This type of scheme, too, would be a step in the direction of structural reform: Such income support would not force farmers to produce unwanted output; acreage payments could be effected whether or not there is any production, or how much; payments could be directly tied to measures for structure improvement and supply management; and they could be capitalized for the purposes indicated above. The system could also be made to correct inequities of exclusive support by price that does not benefit those most in need of support. And it may have good applications in countries other than the EEC, where farm income support has thus far been mainly through price support. In all such cases, the "income-payment" share of farm support could be used to induce structure adjustments that would bring a genuine increase in productivity, and to strengthen desirable social policies.

As in the case of the mixed support system discussed in

* As a matter of arithmetic, the tax in our example would then come to 11 per cent.

the previous section, the purposes and probable effects of
such a policy make it clear that it is a legitimate subject for
the talks on agricultural trade.

Import and Export Obligations and Allocations:
The Concept of Commercial Output

A difficult provision to negotiate for purposes of an international commodity agreement, and later to secure compliance for, is the obligation on importers or exporters to
buy or sell certain guaranteed quantities of the commodity
concerned. In the parlance of international commodity
agreements, such an obligation is the main feature of the
so-called multilateral contract agreement, of which there
is only one practical example—the International Wheat
Agreement during the period 1949 to 1959.* Guarantees
of this kind become operative when prices reach stipulated minimums (import obligation) or maximums (export obligation). Quotas are allocated by country, both for
imports and exports.†

For some commodities, import and export obligations

* For a recent discussion of international commodity arrangements and
policies, see the paper by Gerda Blau presented at the meeting of the
International Economic Association in Vienna, September, 1962, and published in *Monthly Bulletin of Agricultural Economics and Statistics* (FAO,
Rome), XII, September, 1963.

† During the first four-year period—from 1949 to 1953—the Wheat
Agreement covered about two-thirds of the world wheat trade. During
that period, prices on the world market outside the Agreement were
continuously above the maximum stipulated for Agreement trade. In
view of this situation, and since exporters did supply their quotas at
the agreed terms, importers almost fully exercised their right to buy at
the maximum price. During these four years, the agreement thus "operated entirely in the interests of the importers," as Dr. Blau points out. As
soon, however, as the exporters wanted a (modest) increase in the minimum and maximum prices, the United Kingdom and some minor importers withdrew, with the result that "the proportion of world trade
covered . . . dropped to 25 per cent." The idea of guaranteed quantities
was altogether abandoned when the Agreement was renegotiated in 1959.

could, of course, also be part of the content of the agricultural arrangements to be negotiated for a new charter for agriculture under GATT. It has, however, been clear ever since the beginning of the international discussion on the EEC's Common Agricultural Policy that at least some EEC members do not seem to be ready to consider such guarantees.

French leaders and the Commission have made the point that the EEC authorities are not going to guarantee EEC farmers specified quantities of sale; how could they give such guarantees to farmers in outside countries?* Germany, on the other hand, does not seem to be averse to the idea; in fact, recent emphasis on the need to maintain imports from third countries seems to imply an open mind on this question.† Similarly, at least the Netherlands, if not Benelux as a whole, should contemplate the possibility of import guarantees with a measure of sympathy.‡

---

* This, of course, is diplomatic hypocrisy and must not be taken as the last word on the subject. Producers inside the EEC are sufficiently protected by import levies, preferential premiums, export subsidies, and other regulatory devices that virtually assure markets for their products. They need no specific purchase guarantee. Moreover, in the case of the target-price commodities, the EEC rules actually do include purchase obligations at specified intervention prices.

† Mr. Lahr, Under Secretary of the German Foreign Office, feels that the Common Agricultural Policy has up to now not taken sufficient account of the interests of "third countries." Mr. Hüttebräuker, Under Secretary of Agriculture, also expressed his Government's opinion to the effect that the Common Market must assure third countries an appropriate share in the agricultural imports of its members, but has not thus far done so. (Statements made in the EEC Ministerial Council meeting of October 15, 1963). Third-country governments should carefully note these positions.

‡ It is quite hazardous, however, to count on what on the surface may appear as economic interest and common sense. An example for this was offered, in 1962, on the occasion of a discussion of rice in EEC. It would be in the interest of consumers in the Netherlands—and Germany, for example—(with no *direct* producer interest involved there) to be able to maintain imports of the desired long-grain, high-quality product from non-European sources, at low prices. Italy, on the other hand, and to

The idea of export quotas and allocations, on the other hand, is more generally acceptable as a corollary of a "limited" total export market whose size is determined either by agreed import undertakings or announced needs of deficit countries, or by the unregulated impact of a surplus situation in which total commercial requirements fall seriously short of total supplies.* This is only natural, just as

---

some extent France, would not be satisfied to see their producers supported by direct subsidies; they wish to force EEC consumers, through high prices and import barriers, to shift to the lower-quality product grown in Italy and France, and thus permit and even induce expansion of unwanted output. The Netherlands, at that time, made it known quite bluntly that, although much to their distaste, they would support the Italian position in a *quid pro quo* favoring increased exports for Dutch cheese to Italy. It is with some consideration of such "horsetrading" that third countries must try to fathom what kind of international policies the EEC countries might or might not support!

* Such export quotas have, off and on, been in effect—and are now in effect—in a number of instances. The United Kingdom, after an unsuccessful try in GATT at international agreement, since April, 1962, operates a system of import quotas for butter, allocated by countries of origin. This is equivalent to an export-quota arrangement among the exporting countries (with importing-country enforcement assistance), since exporting countries appear to be well satisfied with the equity thus "imposed."

The International Sugar Agreement, up until 1962, was operative as an agreement allocating export shares in the so-called free market. And the International Coffee Agreement ratified in 1963 is an export-quota agreement with the enforcement assistance of importing members.

It is also interesting to note that, before World War II, arrangements having similarity to those now in effect for butter regulated exports of chilled and frozen beef to the United Kingdom. In association with the Livestock Industry Act, 1937, and in agreement with the countries concerned, an International Beef Conference was established, which was representative of the producing interests in the United Kingdom, other Commonwealth countries, and the foreign countries supplying substantial quantities to the United Kingdom market. The Conference, meeting from time to time, drew up allocations for the quantities of beef to be imported from all sources in each quarter of the year. They then divided the quantities among the countries exporting to the United Kingdom, taking into account any quantities that were required for allocation to any particular country—e.g., Argentina—under Treaty obligations. An essential feature of the arrangement was that the allocations had to be agreed on unanimously. Any country was free to refuse to accept the allocation proposed for it by the Conference. In that event, however, the whole matter had to

it would be natural for importing countries readily to accept import obligations and allocations in the case of shortages.

In both instances, the essential idea is one of "equitable sharing" (of "limited" markets or "limited" supplies), which is, however, only *part* of the essential idea of commodity arrangements of the multilateral contract type and, especially, of the type now desirable to help in a reconciliation of agricultural support with reasonable maintenance of trade.

What is now needed clearly includes specified import and export commitments, or specified contributions to giveaway programs of food aid, and definite obligations with respect to domestic policy to support a smooth functioning of those external commitments: in the case of both importing and exporting countries, to control domestic output (and/or agree to domestic financing of specified contributions to giveaway programs); and to maintain carry-over stocks for elasticity and flexibility on a world scale; and also, in the case of exporting countries, to maintain readiness for expansion for any sudden emergence of additional commercial or noncommercial needs.

It is at this point of our discussion that the concept of commercial output suggests itself. We know from many an instructive international experience that success in arriving at agreements is made up to the extent of, say, one-half, of material provisions; the other half is psychology. If

---

be referred back to the Board of Trade, which, in conformity with the provisions of the Livestock Industry Act, would make the allocations as it thought fit. That the Conference worked satisfactorily is borne out by the fact that, throughout the period of its operation, agreement was always reached. The arrangement was suspended with the onset of World War II. (Information supplied by L. A. Wheeler, Director of the North American office of the International Federation of Agricultural Producers.)

direct import undertakings are difficult to obtain, perhaps another method of achieving a more secure maintenance of trade would prove more acceptable. To explain what I have in mind I must briefly revert to M. Pisani's Plan for international trade.

As we have seen, M. Pisani hopes that demand supplementation by international give-away programs can substitute for the lost function of prices. In this he appears to overestimate the absorption capacity of such programs. On the other hand, his plan is weak in regard to effective management of the supply side of the equation, especially where France is concerned. These are, however, shortcomings that could be corrected. It should be possible to devise arrangements that would not only give supply management a place of equal importance with demand supplementation, *but would even interlock these two programs.* Where firm direct trade undertakings do not seem feasible, international agreement might include an understanding on "commercial-output quotas."

The idea is that, if governments agree to reserve for noncommercial disposal, out of domestic output, all quantities, say, of grain produced over and above a basic commercial quota, this would be just as effective as a guarantee of international trade quotas and might prove psychologically and politically more acceptable.

Basic annual quotas for commercial output might be agreed upon for moving three-year periods, with flexible annual renegotiation provisions if trade develops contrary to the agreed purpose, which should be a reasonable development of domestic output and of international trade. Negotiated individual-country quotas would define the concept "reasonable" in concrete terms and could permit expansion in some countries, while providing for contrac-

said, aims, in the first place, to gain from a relocation of production toward a more economical pattern *within* the union area, not from diverting trade away from third countries. However, the circumstances we are facing in the EEC make it quite probable that, unmitigated, they would tend to obviate internal relocation at the expense of imports from outside the area.

Obligatory import quotas might prevent this tendency, but only so far as the size of imports is concerned and hence without protecting against the dangerous pressures of contrary production policies; commercial-output quotas, on the other hand, would tend to promote internal relocation more fully and more directly. For it is obvious that this well-known and essential principle of economic union —increased productivity from relocations—would cry for a place in an agreed internal EEC allocation of such output quotas. Economic common sense, international trade, and reasonable types of agricultural support would profit from such an influence.

Import Targets: Inducements for Compliance

Ideas that can be advanced under this heading might aim at some compromise between the principles of a system of tariff quotas (to suggest which, as I have said before, so far as the EEC is concerned, would be quite unrealistic and naïve) and a system of import guarantees. I touch upon this method not because I think it is likely to prove practicable, but rather for the sake of completeness—and just in case, by some quirk of fate, it *might* prove negotiable as well as promising.

The idea would simply be that importing countries, including the EEC, would accept negotiated import targets with government obligation to vary whatever protection

tion of *commercial* (not necessarily *total*) output elsewhere.

A system of this kind would have enough flexibility to accommodate opposite interests within the limits of reason. It would link the inseparable components of demand supplementation and supply control—inseparable components of deliberate management where price has been largely deprived of its equilibrating function. France in particular, where the Pisani Plan assigns food aid such a central technical and moral role in the management of the markets, could not very well oppose the idea *that governments should make definite commitments* for putting supplies into the food-aid pool, if only to the extent that their countries happen to produce more than allotted shares in commercial markets. And having so loudly proclaimed an ethical imperative for the developed world to feed the needy populations from its abundance, France could not in good grace exempt herself from a contribution commensurate with its agricultural capacity and with its role as a great moral and economic power.

Flexibility would also be afforded by the three-year provision. Under it, a production shortfall in one year, for example, could be offset in the next two, thus permitting a correction of overimportation or underexportation. Provision could be made for letting the corrective development take place at the expense of the beneficiaries of the previous imbalance.

In offering the idea of negotiated commercial-output quotas I do not mean to suggest that, for some commodities, specific import and export obligations could not be negotiated. On the contrary, I think that a variety of possibilities must be explored. The system of commercial-output quotas could also be combined with a system exclusively of commercial-export quotas for the exporting countries, without output quotas. Fantastic as it may seem at first, even a mixed system of commercial-output quotas for some countries, obligatory import quotas for others, and export quotas for still others might prove feasible, for they all can be reduced to shares in the total commercial market.*

If it should prove desirable to give the underdeveloped countries in need of food aid assurances on a minimum level and types of such noncommercial supplies, provisions of this kind could be made part of the negotiations and ensuing agreements. I mention this point because several advocates of effective international agreements have insisted that noncommercial trade should be included in the forthcoming negotiations. There is no reason why it should not.

In the case of EEC, the question will arise as to whether import (and/or export) obligations or output quotas should be negotiated by and for the individual member countries or by and for the Community as such, and whether the resulting giveaway burden should be financed by the treasuries of the individual member countries or out of Community funds.

On a number of occasions I have argued that quotas will have to be assumed or agreed to by the individual member governments, and that resulting burdens should be correspondingly financed. My thought here was, above all, that individual-country financing would be more equitable and would constitute a certain amount of pressure toward more reasonable production policies. This is not

* The counterpart of commercial-output quotas or shares in the commercial market is, of course, an implicit allocation or donation of supplies for stocking and aid—the noncommercial market. It is conceivable that the whole idea could in practice assume the form of a financial pool to which importing as well as exporting countries would contribute and from which this surplus disposal would be financed. Such a system, however, is not at this time a likely prospect—although, as such, it would be feasible and would perhaps even have greater merit.

much of a point to argue about, however, if the EEC within its own ranks, can achieve agreement on how to distribute internally the privileges and burdens resulting from Community-wide commitments and Community wide financing. Yet, there is a bit of a problem there.

It is perhaps probable that the EEC will insist on an approach in which the Community would appear as on unit. In that case it would seem necessary for the EEC to have some suballocations of commitments among the member countries. Suppose the Community were to guarantee total imports of grains and that this guarantee would amount to x million tons for a given year. The determination of such a quantity, no doubt, will have been based on definite quantitative assumptions by countries as to how much of their production would be regarded as "commercial output," how much they would presumably produce altogether, and how much would thus be expected to result as "noncommercial output" for Community or national stocking and/or later disposition in aid programs. these quantities for stocking and/or aid were to be financed by the respective national treasuries, overproduction in some member countries would matter little to the other members. If, however, financing had to come out Community funds, the situation would obviously be quite different.

As a final comment on obligatory trade quotas and commercial output quotas I would like to say that, compared with straight undertakings on imports and exports, commercial-output method would seem to have something to commend itself, quite aside from the advantages that might thus far have emerged from our discussion. I have reference to one of the principles of economic integration to which I alluded before.* The true customs union

* Cf. p. 19 ff. above.

exists at the frontier to a sufficient extent (which may or may not be quite small) to create the incentive necessary to induce the private trade to bring in the target quantities.

I am not very hopeful that this method would prove more nearly compatible with the EEC system of price support than would the traditional tariff-quota system; or that, if more nearly compatible, it would prove effective in realizing the targets. But it is perhaps useful to note that, in the GATT negotiations of 1960–62 and again in the U.K.–EEC negotiations formulas were advanced that touched upon something akin to the import-target concept. I have particularly in mind the proposal that, in the event of a substantial decline in its imports as a result of the Common Agricultural Policy, the EEC would take "appropriate measures" to remedy the decline. Aside from a longer-term control of output, the most readily conceivable remedial measures would be purchases by a Community market organization (or Community-coordinated country agencies) for stocking or aid disposals, or the creation of the necessary inducements to imports by the private trade to reach the "targets."

Miscellaneous Provisions

There will be other matters that should be included in the discussions of proposals for agreements. Some will emerge as corollaries to the important subjects that have been mentioned. But there will be still others.

For commodities that would not be included in price agreements, and for which *minimum import prices* (also called gate prices, lock-gate prices, or reference prices) would still seem essential to governments of importing areas, the new Code for Agriculture should provide for their application in strict conformity with the idea of emergency action under the antidumping philosophy of GATT's Articles VI and XIX.

If *export subsidies* must continue in some countries, they would have to be strictly subject to the "equitable-export-shares" provisions of GATT's Article XVI. For the commodities placed under an international agreement, a quantitative definition of this vague term would automatically result. For other commodities, a more concrete definition should also be secured.

Fixed Tariffs or Tariff-Free Entry

It is generally agreed that international commodity arrangements would only be suitable for some products—grains, possibly meat, some dairy products, sugar. For others, fixed tariffs should remain the only form of protection; for still others, imports would not be dutiable at all. For commodities that are of more sectional interest and do not represent the same all-inclusive problem of agriculture as a whole as does the grain-livestock economy, this approach is either already in being or represents a definite possibility.

In the EEC, tobacco, fruits, fruit juices, and vegetables, oil-seeds and vegetable oil, and some minor livestock products belong in this category. (Other products could be added, although some of those mentioned may be withdrawn and placed under more restrictive systems.) EEC partners should, with priority, seek agreement in the negotiations on the range of the products for which fixed tariffs or tariff-free entry should remain the rule. The United States, in particular, should carefully avoid a doctrinaire approach in these cases, despite the temptations of the Trade Expansion Act. A decision, for example, to press for tariff reductions on sensitive items might prove fatal for the purpose of keeping them in the fixed-tariff category.* To be willing or even eager to suggest the greatest possible number of items for inclusion in sweeping tariff reductions on all sides is one thing; to be adamant in difficult cases would be quite another.

Recapitulation

I shall try briefly to recapitulate and perhaps amplify in some respects the suggestions for details of what might be a realistic compromise.

The negotiations on agriculture, for or in the Kennedy Round, should aim to write a code for agricultural support and trade. This code would be embodied in a number of individual commodity agreements and one over-all agreement covering general aspects and provisions that would not find an appropriate place in the commodity parts.

All GATT countries would be signatories; non-GATT countries could also accede; special provisions for less developed countries would be included. In setting our sights in this manner we will have taken a step toward dealing constructively also with issues that will be on the agenda of the United Nations Conference on Trade and Development.

The code would be grounded in a generally acceptable basic philosophy and resultant broad principles. Individual commodity agreements will be concluded for grains (transforming the International Wheat Agreement into a more inclusive compact of different type); for beef and possibly other kinds of fresh and frozen meat; for butter, dried whole and skim milk; and for sugar. There may be

---

* For a concrete example of this type, see Chapter 7, p. 44 ff.

consideration of additional commodities, under second priority.

Specifically, partly depending upon the commodity, elements of the agreements will be related to international prices and/or price ranges; internal prices in importing and exporting countries; direct producer payments by products and/or as global income supports tied to purposes of direct supply control, longer-term structural reform, and/or social assistance; obligatory minimum import and export quotas and allocations; programs of demand supplementation, especially through a system of commercial-output quotas with conditional obligations for contributions in kind to stocking and food-aid schemes or contributions to a money pool for financing stocking and food aid; stocking policies as such and internationalization of food aid; agreements on fixed tariffs for selected products; and the application of traditional GATT rules and procedures to such provisions as minimum import prices and export subsidies.

In the case of grains, most of these elements may apply. For butter, countries might just aim at agreed export-quota allocations for imports into the United Kingdom and some other regular importing countries, possibly coupled with agreed minimum-maximum prices and commercial-output quotas, at least in importing countries.

For nonfat dry milk, and part-skim and whole-milk powder, an agreement should stipulate minimum-maximum prices and should allocate export quotas by individual exporting countries. This commodity may also call for a special arrangement to secure sufficient contributions to an international food-aid program for free supplies to less developed countries. The commercial-output idea might, in this case, be supplemented by the allocation of total-output goals to *all* developed countries that are significant dairy producers, to make sure of a continuity of adequate aid supplies for the poor areas where there is still a great unfilled need.*

For meat, further detailed study is required to obtain more positive indications of what is desirable and feasible. As a beginning, export quotas allocated by countries may have to suffice. As in the case of butter, the United Kingdom has made a practical start with voluntary import allocations, agreed with supplying countries, for bacon, coupled with a domestic supply quota—something akin to our commercial-output concept.

Financing of some of the supports—say, of demand supplementation through commercial-output quotas and resultant contributions to free food aid—might also be an item for negotiation, although it will more likely be left to the discretion of the individual partner countries.

With respect to the commercial-output concept, we should keep in mind that it has far-reaching ramifications: It makes supply control a responsibility of governments rather than of individual farmers and, because of this and its link to demand supplementation, it is less problematical, easier to enforce, and no more difficult to defend than supply control at the farm level. It also permits a stocking policy and food-aid activities (both with foreign-policy implications) of greater elasticity. Like producer subsidies tied to supply control, it can be used to implement or facilitate the realization of the basic principle not to increase protection further. On the other hand, it may not per-

---

* At its Conference at New Delhi in 1959, the International Federation of Agricultural Producers (IFAP), in an explanatory statement preceding its resolution on a Food and Farm Policy, indicated alarm at the interruption of the flow of supplies to needy areas and urged early preparation of measures that would assure a continuity of supplies of dry skim milk for distribution in less developed countries. (The United States had, at that time, suspended deliveries because of depletion of stocks.)

manently avoid the need for contractual farmer participation in such supply control.

As to a flexible policy on stocks, we must remember that governments joining in a deliberate effort at such management cannot avoid assuming considerable responsibility for the availability at all times of adequate food supplies to meet all effective demand, and of the noncommercial needs to provide a share that should at least not diminish. The more well-to-do countries, and perhaps even the less well-to-do with large export interests in a given commodity, will therefore need to round out their agreements by a well-defined policy on reserve stocks.

The recent events in the international grain markets, with the sudden appearance of large import demands by the U.S.S.R. and East European countries plus the import requirements of Communist China, clearly show the need for a well-considered reserve policy. And aside from these developments—which may or may not continue, may or may not reflect longer-term factors and policies—there are some long-term influences that reinforce this need.

An outstanding agricultural economist warned us three years ago that "despite the abundance of the present supply on the markets of the Western world of grains and livestock products, we must not lose sight of the possibility that these . . . circumstances . . . might in the longer run change. Symptoms of this possibility are the exodus of the young people from agriculture in the industrial countries, the rapid population increase outside Western Europe, and the potential political pressure of malnutrition in the densely populated areas of the less developed world."* Although he added that, for the time being, these

---

* Arthur Hanau, "Die Deutsche Veredlungswirtschaft in Rahmen der EWG," in *Tierernährung und Tierhaltung* (Hamburg: Lohmann & Co., 1961).

influences are remote and that for the immediate future the Western world's worry will center on surpluses, the warning conveniently emphasizes the other side of international rules for agriculture and trade; these rules should cautiously contemplate the tomorrow as much as the today.

13. Britain Prepares

AMONG THE countries most interested in international trade in agricultural products—positively or negatively—Australia and New Zealand have perhaps shown the greatest zeal in pressing for practicable accommodations. Canada has been, and still is, the most skeptical regarding new arrangements; possessing an export product, such as its quality wheat, that is hard to beat and still in secure demand, Canadians fear that experimenting with new schemes might do more harm than good.

The Government of France was the first and the most alert to come forward with a plan for agricultural trade, albeit in somewhat unofficial terms. Messrs. Pisani and Baumgartner lost no time in November, 1961, in using a highly appropriate FAO and GATT occasion to throw out some interesting ideas for debate and negotiation. The United States, on the other hand, although it has been the most vociferous in proclaiming the need for effective arrangements on agriculture, without which the Kennedy negotiations would end in failure, has made no concrete suggestions, put forward no plan, and has not even responded to other countries' proposals with detailed analysis and discussion. And it is largely because of this lack of vigorous initiative and response on the part of the United States that the present status of our international dialogue on concrete programs is so unsatisfactory. The stereotyped calls for "access" to markets in importing countries, or for a chance "to compete fairly," are no substitute for a concrete plan.

In the meantime, the British Government has been quietly preparing for the day. Its role in the negotiations with the EEC was pre-eminent, and many of the constructive proposals on which agreement between the EEC and the U.K. was reached or in sight had been largely British contributions. It was in their nature that they looked to world-wide applications.

Since the collapse of these talks, Britain has taken further significant steps to move into position for constructive participation in world-wide negotiations on a new international code for agriculture and agricultural trade. Characteristically determined to put up with the inevitable and, having lost out on a specific issue, to seek next-best solutions, Great Britain has prepared to equip itself both with a new program and with the tools to join in an international effort.

A government that, in February, 1962 (when a Geneva session on grain gingerly touched upon the Pisani Plan), would not even consider talking about the implications of a possible agreed increase in international grain prices, has resolutely turned its back upon the idea of cheapest imports at any price, so to speak. It now advocates minimum import prices from which exporters may be permitted to profit, depending upon the content of world-wide agreements yet to be negotiated. The wisdom of any such change will in part be determined by its extent; but the implied flexibility of policy is in any case remarkable.

The modifications that the Government of the United Kingdom now proposes to introduce in its system of agricultural support and trade are, of course, not exclusively motivated by considerations of trade policy. They must be seen against the program as hitherto operated.

Since the end of the war, Britain's farm support, laid

down in comprehensive legislation, aims at profitable home production of a major share of the country's total food requirements and at importing the remaining needs at the lowest possible prices. The system, in general, provides for a domestic price level for food at low import parities, while farm incomes are protected by direct deficiency payments on commodities and by production grants not tied to specific products. The system is open-ended in the sense that it does not carry limitations on output or on the producer payments that stimulated output. As a result, production increased by formidable proportions, and so did the Treasury costs of farm support.

For quite some time past, the Government has indicated its desire to stabilize home production, and guaranteed prices have been adjusted downward. More stringent control of domestic output, however, seemed to be necessary. At the same time, control of imports appeared as a logical corollary of output control and desirable also with a view to international initiatives.

On May 22, 1963, the Minister of Agriculture stated in the House of Commons that the Government intended to control imports and import prices as well as domestic output of cereals and fatstock. The intention is, briefly, to maintain a reasonable degree of farm support, but not to encourage unlimited production;* thus to limit the Government's liability for the costs of farm support and to maintain imports at reasonable levels, and also to have effective machinery to assure Commonwealth and other traditional suppliers of acceptable shares in Britain's trade

---

* Support is to be limited to "standard quantities" of output. There is some kinship between this concept and the French "quantum" concept (for wheat) and my concept of "commercial output"—with obvious policy implications. The standard quantity, in British terminology, is the quantity of a product that the Government considers desirable and reasonable to have produced at home.

through participation in international agreements or otherwise.

There is no doubt that such a change in British policy will serve as much as a safeguard against policies of the Common Market that might injure the interests of the Commonwealth and third countries on the British market as to facilitate Britain's participation in joint approaches with the EEC and in general international coordination. Beyond that, the change will open further possibilities for cooperation, not to say association, with EEC and other countries by adoption of mixed support-price–producer-subsidy schemes toward which the EEC also moves; and by the acceptance of the idea of negotiated international (and hence import) prices such as M. Pisani had suggested.*

It will be recalled (see p. 112, footnote) that since April, 1962, Britain allocates to exporting countries specific shares in its market for butter. Since the Minister's statement of May 22, 1963, the Government has moved further in getting ready for international negotiations not unlike those envisioned in the present review. It has submitted proposals to Britain's overseas suppliers of cereals and meat featuring minimum import prices as well as quantitative arrangements. With respect to bacon, agreement has already been reached for a sharing of markets in the United Kingdom between British agriculture and foreign suppliers, largely based on traditional patterns of supply.

* In a letter to the editor of the *Times* of London published on March 19, 1963, I proposed a potentially happy compromise between the EEC moving from a mere support-price system to a mixed one supplemented by producer payments, and Britain moving to the same mixed system from the other end. My suggestions did not stop there, but also envisioned the selection of the French price level for basic products as that for immediately unified market and support prices in both Britain and the EEC—supplemented, where desirable, by producer payments. The present British proposals keep the door open for this additional choice, although after the EEC Commission's higher grain-price proposals of November 5, it would be difficult to get the French price accepted.

With this, Britain is already moving quietly ahead, setting an example of what is sometimes called a pragmatic approach. It is also understood that these steps are first feelers and that the British Government intends to keep an open mind on modifications of its new arrangements and proposals. If this is the attitude, it should help in preparing for realistic negotiations in Geneva. At the same time, there would be no premature commitment to the more problematic ranges of price and quantity ideas that have been aired.

14. The Issue Restated

In this brief analysis I hope to have shown that our problem, although complex, does not necessarily defy attempts at solution. As we have also seen, our work on it has at times been inadequate, and we must improve on past performance. The negotiators of all governments must be well grounded in the theory, history, and practice of trade policy, and, while acting as dependable spokesmen of their countries, must be imbued with the spirit of give and take and with humility toward the interests of all. Truly, ours is not only a job of analysis, but also one of education.

Once again I should like to emphasize that the twin problem of agricultural protection and trade has developed over a long time, has its roots in facts of our economic and social life, and has not been created by the plans and policies of regional integration. But the emergence of the EEC has added to the problem and has made it urgent for governments to settle on a policy for agriculture in the context of international cooperation.

Even if Britain were never to join the EEC, or the EEC itself were not to survive, some of its policy plans and methods will. And the need for an agreed international policy on agriculture in GATT would still require an early settlement.

A word of caution is in order on prospects for production and trade. First, there can be no question that "outside" agricultural exporters will suffer to some extent from the effects of EEC integration. The complete preference accorded trade within the area—an inescapable effect of economic union—in the circumstances of the member countries *must* have this consequence. The question is only to what *extent* it will affect outside trade.

Second, even without the emergence of a common market in Europe, agricultural production would probably continue to increase, perhaps even more rapidly than requirements. The role of such factors as low population growth, demand elasticities, and the impact of technology have been pointed out.

Technological progress includes advances made in plant and animal breeding, in fertilizer use, in feeding, pasture management, cultivation, and plant protection; and it also includes mechanization releasing acreage previously used for the production of feed for draft animals—a process still in full swing in Europe. All these improvements continue to spread more and more from the more advanced enterprises into the broader group of average farms. Processes of structural reform will even accelerate this trend.

There are thus facts that have already been accepted, and tendencies that cannot, or not in any significant degree, be influenced by international initiatives. One might even say, paradoxically, that in the relatively near future, the growth of commercial agricultural trade is likely to be hampered either by the growth of protection or by the growth of productivity. Clearly, the world's choice must be for the latter. But in any case, it will be the better part of wisdom for all agricultural exporting countries of the temperate zone to face this prospect realistically in their negotiations as well as in their international and domestic policies.

The problem today is to make possible the peaceful coexistence of inevitable protection of agriculture in many lands with a reasonable volume of agricultural trade. We believe to have, at least in the Western world, a basic economic and social philosophy conducive to viable compromise. And from this philosophy follow some broad principles, reasonably acceptable to all, that should help in reaching an agreement in concrete and workable terms.

Among the broad principles that might guide us is the acknowledgment that we must proceed with economic common sense, though it cannot be the sole determinant of our policies; that further increases in artificial protection must be avoided, except in serious emergencies; that, if we deprive price of its equilibrating function, we must seek some other management of supply as well as of demand; and that we must give definite commitments on domestic policies to achieve the international purposes we pursue.

With respect to the principle of "no further increase in protection," we should not seek quantitative *measurements* of such protection, which then might be bound at stated levels. Instead, we should concentrate on agreement to limit the *results* of protection. These efforts are more likely to succeed if they are supported by reasonable price arrangements that pull in the desired direction.

Such arrangements will at the same time benefit the management of supply and demand which we should seek primarily through the establishment of a link between the two. Its effectiveness might be aided by emphasizing government, rather than individual, action. The link should be a logical as well as a moral one—thus compelling in two respects. On the logical side, the concept of commercial output would ease supply control through demand supplementation by government responsibility for the disposal of production in excess of commercial output. On the moral side, those who emphasize the developed countries' obligation to help feed the needy areas cannot simply claim a right to *producing* such supplies while shirking the obligation of also *contributing* them to that purpose.

Finally, in contemplating an international compact or commodity agreements, we must not let ourselves be over-awed or discouraged by the obvious difficulties in prospect. Thus far, it is true, efforts at international commodity agreements have not been too successful; and even market-ing agreements between producers in one and the same country have often had a history of failure and frustration. However, if we despair at the thought, what else is there that we can do, other than just wait and hope for the best? Also, we must not envisage international agreements to require negotiations of monstrous proportions promis-ing little beyond idle talk and recrimination. Modest be-ginnings and gradual approaches are, of course, the rea-sonable middle course. For example, the arrangements on butter and bacon that the United Kingdom has quietly made and put into effect are steps in the right direction. They can be amplified and modified and then may serve as an arrangement of the needed kind, so far as these commodities are concerned.

Furthermore, we must not be overawed by the specific difficulty of getting agreement on market sharing between domestic production and imports. Such sharing is not with-out precedents. It is, for example, a feature of those recent arrangements between the United Kingdom and supplying countries; and it has for long been agreed practice in the Sugar Act programs of the United States, which assure foreign suppliers a definite proportion of total U.S. de-mand. There are other examples as well.

In fact, whichever way we place the emphasis, interna-tional policies on our problem will always imply a sharing of responsibilities among importing and exporting coun-tries. They imply international sharing of the burdens that result from our efforts to maintain reasonable protection of farm incomes—that is to say, from the support policies in importing as well as exporting countries. They imply a sharing, by all, of commercial and noncommercial markets; a sharing of the resource returns still accessible to agriculture; and cooperation in the positive contribution into which noncommercial disposal may be transformed in alleviating need and in assisting economic development in the poorer areas of the world.

In weighing the chances of an international accommodation on agricultural policies and trade, we should also remember that a number of proposals and actions can now be drawn upon, and that these proposals and actions have many points in common. They have fed on each other. Especially certain parts of the Pisani Plan have proved an all-pervading influence; and much of it runs through later suggestions by other parties. It runs through what had developed as a set of points agreed in the EEC–U.K. negotiations; through the EEC Commission's proposals for the GATT negotiations on agriculture; through the recent initiatives of the British Government; and through the proposals of the International Chamber of Commerce. Suggestions in the plans of other countries or organizations have similarly found favor with each other's sponsors. Thus the stage seems to be set for negotiations of reasonable intent and scope. But we do need patience and perseverance, clear thought and courage, to strike a realistic bargain.

Despite all this we must always be prepared for defeat. It is, as I said, entirely possible that all such efforts will come to naught, that satisfactory agreements on an international policy for agriculture will at this time prove impossible of achievement. Such an outcome could have serious consequences. It is for this reason that we must make an earnest try.

APPENDIX

I. THE STORY OF THE GERMAN
DUTY ON ORANGES

THE EEC Treaty obligates Germany gradually to raise its import duty on oranges from 10 to 16 per cent; a first-step increase has already been effected. It has been calculated that the full increase will cost the German consumer an additional outlay of more than $10 million.

In requesting an exemption from its obligation (or a sizable import quota at the original 10 per cent tariff), the German Government pointed out that a higher tariff would not benefit Italy (the only orange producer in EEC), because its output was too small to meet total EEC requirements. A higher tariff would raise prices to German consumers on a total quantity of imports many times larger than the quantity on which Italian producers could book a profit. (Germany's imports from Italy in 1959–61 amounted to one-half of Italian exports, which still was only 12 per cent of total German imports.)

After the Commission had refused the request, the

European Court, on an appeal by the German Government, ruled for the Commission. The Court was of the opinion that continued importation by Germany of oranges from third countries at a tariff of 10 per cent might impair the sales possibilities, at reasonable prices, of EEC-produced apples, pears, and peaches; and that off-season sales possibilities for EEC apples might be increased through appropriate storage facilities, provided Germany is not granted the requested low-tariff orange contingent.

This ruling, in effect, implies that the EEC's agricultural policy has discretion to induce consumers to eat EEC apples and pears in place of Spanish or Israeli oranges. From this kind of policy there is only a short step to making people consume EEC pork in place of imported beef or poultry, or to similar substitutions. Commissioner Mansholt has little reason, indeed, to protest, as he did on a visit to Washington, D.C., against the description of the Common Market's agricultural policy as "protectionist and inward-looking." (*Foreign Agriculture,* April 22, 1963, p. 4.)

In reporting the above situation, the *Neue Zürcher Zeitung* of August 3, 1963 (Foreign ed., No. 211, p. 3), points out how different the attitudes of France and Italy are vis-à-vis Switzerland. The paper wonders what their protest would be if Switzerland were to discontinue its imports of peaches or oranges on the ground that there were sufficient supplies of domestic apricots or apples.

II. MEASURING DEGREES OF
SUPPORT OR PROTECTION

IN PROPOSING the acceptance of the principle "no further increase in protection"—and believing that this, in fact, is a negotiable principle—we do not necessarily imply that degrees of protection or support could actually be measured. What we do imply, however, is that we can or could identify those changes in protective measures and policies or developments that would either increase or reduce protection.

Obvious increases in protection, for example, would be increases in support prices in real terms or in relation to input costs, increases in direct producer payments not offset by increased costs, increases in subsidies to reduce the costs of input items, increases in export subsidies that would either raise unit returns to producers or increase sales volume, and so forth.

Not all such cases would be easy to determine, especially if there is a substitution of one type of measure for another, or relaxation of one for tightening of another. But in general there would be no serious disagreement among expert observers. A general undertaking, with respect to agriculture as a whole, of "no further increases in protection"—subject, if necessary, to an emergency exemption —would, therefore, be a provision that could be administered and enforced.

In its proposals for the GATT negotiations on agriculture, the EEC Commission suggests the negotiation and binding of support levels or levels of protection (*montants* *de soutien*) with regard to individual products. This, in fact, would presuppose the possibility of quantitative measurement of the levels of protection or degrees of support.*

The Commission's proposals, in most cases, would appear to boil down to a simple binding of support prices. However, in view of many additional elements of support other than product prices, concentration on price alone would not in fact represent total protection. This would not be satisfactory; and if those other elements could be included at all, they could only be included on highly controversial bases of calculation; they could hardly be allocated to individual products.

The proposed binding of degrees of protection through binding of prices would not be satisfactory for yet another reason: It proposes to start from a level of protection that is already considerably above what should, in fact, be held unchanged. (The level proposed by the Commission for the unified grain price is in this category.) And there is still a further difficulty.

A commitment by countries not to increase protection would be one thing; a binding of a specific *montant de soutien* or amount of support, quite another. The former commitment could be measured against objective criteria easy to understand and comparatively easy to determine: Output increases within specified limits—the concept of commercial output could help here—or commercial imports (or exports) constant or in constant proportions to total commercial requirements (or output). If these conditions were to prevail, they would be accepted as proof of compliance with the undertaking not to increase protection. Such compliance would still reserve for farmers in the countries concerned the results of increases in their own productivity so far as they can be reaped without increases

* Cf. p. 92 above.

in commercial output beyond the limits set by the agreed criterion.* And there is quite a bit of room for increases in income as a result of increases in productivity without or with limited expansion of total output: With farm prices fixed or otherwise controlled, and total supply controlled, increases in productivity would automatically be reflected in higher incomes (rather than lower prices).

On the other hand, binding of a specific amount of support, if it could be done at all comprehensively, would require a quantification, not of the results of protection (which alone matter), but of protection itself—an almost impossible task. And it would set no limit beyond which increases in income should exclusively be derived from increases in output per unit of input rather than from increases in output displacing or diverting trade.

As I have said before, we should favor a pragmatic approach with respect to the undertaking not to increase protection. The decisive criterion would be the development of trade; and bindings would realistically relate to that rather than to amounts of protection. Realistically, again, this type of binding could be made tight or loose; for trade to be maintained, increased, or reduced—differentially, by countries; of exports as well as imports; and so forth. True, elements of rigidity are introduced by such a system, and economical resource utilization may not only be promoted, but in some respects may suffer. To some extent, however, this is unavoidable; we cannot interfere with the price system and the market economy without sacrificing some of their advantages—and we do this in

* Increases in productivity would thus, not illogically, be recognized as the main source from which the desired improvement in agricultural incomes would have to come. (I say "main" source because special disbursements of a social character may well be stepped up in a number of countries.)

order to gain others. There is no magic here with which we could hope to square the circle.

In concluding these notes on the measurement of degrees of protection, I think it would be useful to allude to the general problem posed by the idea of such measurements. I had occasion to express some views on this problem in connection with GATT's report on *Trends in International Trade* (Geneva, October, 1958). The panel of experts that wrote this report had recommended that GATT and FAO make a study, for various countries, to measure the degrees of agricultural protection.* I pointed out at the time that attempts in this direction had been made before by a number of economists.† Thus, Erik Swedborg and Karl Säkk measured the degrees to which farm prices in various countries exceed the import prices—excluding duties—for comparable products.‡ Hans Bachmann and Wilhelm Gasser, in Switzerland, were not satisfied with a simple calculation of the costs of farm support for their country—the sum total of all direct and indirect subsidies plus the difference between domestic farm prices and import prices, excluding duty; they also calculated the cost of

* It was, partly, as a result of this suggestion that GATT's Committee II asked the GATT and FAO secretariats to make such calculations, with guidance by a study group of government economists acting in the capacity of professional experts. The study group also was to assemble and sift the calculations and to pass judgment on the merits of the job and of the underlying idea. The work was never finished; a decidedly pessimistic view as to the possibility of finding satisfactory methods and the usefulness of "measuring" prevailed in the study group, in the two secretariats, and in the professional circles of the governments that had been asked to help with materials and otherwise. The study group thus far has made no "assessment of the feasibility" of the proposed method of calculation. This is the "work in GATT Committee II" to which the Mansholt suggestions for binding *montants de soutien* referred hopefully.

† See J. H. Richter, "Trends in International Trade," in *Quarterly Journal of Economics,* November, 1959. In describing the wider problem, I draw, in part, on that article (with permission of the *Journal* and of the Harvard University Press).

‡ *Prissättningen På Jordbruksprodukter,* Appendix 6 (Stockholm, 1954).

existing protection in the other segments of the economy. A comparison of real incomes as they existed with those that would have obtained if there had been no protection for either industry or agriculture yielded the startling result that, under such circumstances, the farmers' real income would, in 1949–50, have been higher than it actually was under all-around protection. (In 1935–38, it would have been the same.)*

Similarly, Professor Austin Robinson, long a student of "the cost of agricultural import-saving," was not merely interested in measuring the degree of agricultural protection in the United Kingdom. Setting his sights upon a far more pertinent approach, one still more inclusive than that of Bachmann and Gasser, he directed his efforts toward answering the question whether a reduction in agricultural protection could appreciably add to the real income of the United Kingdom population at large.†

In taking such an approach it is, of course, necessary to form some quantitative judgment of what the prices would be, in the long run, at which supplies could be obtained (and sold) in the international market if all supports—import charges, export subsidies, other subsidies, and producer payments—were removed. Graham Hallett devoted some work to such calculations or "reasonable guesses," so far as protection of British agriculture is concerned.‡

In efforts to determine degrees of protection or sup-

* Cf. Hans Bachmann and Wilhelm Gasser, *Die Volkswirtschaftlich Optimale Nutzung des Schweizer Bodens* (Zurich and St. Gallen, 1956), and *Agrarpolitik und Aussenwirtschaft* (St. Gallen, 1948). A later study, for more recent years, showed results similar to those obtained for 1949–50. Some of the calculations were challenged in a study by H. Wilbrandt, *Die Regulierung des Milchmarktes in der Schweiz* (Kieler Studien, Kiel, 1956), pp. 244 ff.

† Austin Robinson, "The Cost of Agricultural Import-Saving," *The Three Banks Review*, December, 1958.

‡ Cf. his article, "The Economic Position of British Agriculture," in *The Economic Journal*, September, 1959.

port, simple computations of the differences between farm prices and import or export prices, plus subsidies paid, does not, therefore, suffice. For the real question is: How economic a use are countries making of their *total* resources of land, labor, and capital?

In view of the problem at hand, the first step toward an answer to this question might be taken through an inquiry to determine whether an elimination or moderation of agricultural protection could, *ceteris paribus,* improve total resource allocation and thus raise the real income of a country's population. An affirmative answer would establish a tentative presumption that the extent of the existing agricultural support is damaging to the country concerned, and that it is also damaging internationally, for the reason that uneconomical resource allocation in one open economy must of necessity be paralleled by uneconomical resource allocation in others. And "paralleled" may mean "caused by" or "the cause of" or a condition of functional interdependence in which the situations in all countries feed upon each other. Conversely, a negative answer would establish a tentative presumption that the extent of existing agricultural support is not damaging.

Conclusions thus arrived at would be only tentative, because of the *ceteris paribus* assumption: If nothing were to change, or could be changed, in other segments of the economy concerned or, for that matter, in other economies. Further steps in such an analysis, therefore, would have to contemplate a similar inquiry, first, with respect to other segments of the economy concerned. For it is obvious that an increase or decrease of protection in other industries might in itself mean a decrease or increase in the "real" extent of existing agricultural protection and, hence, of the comparative profitability of agricultural production as against industrial production in the country concerned

—with the reverse result in other countries. And additional inquiries would have to ferret out information on other countries also. It is clear that the extent of import-saving induced by agricultural protection in country A might or might not, at least in part, be a function of other countries' industrial protection that would preclude country A's exporting more industrial goods to pay for larger agricultural imports. There are still other ramifications and interrelationships that would have to be examined; I mention only the crucial point that it is not so much what other segments and other countries do now as what they might do in the future that plays a role in this context.

It is also obvious that the complexity of studies of this kind would defy all attempts at quantitative approaches. And yet this is the only kind of analysis that would be theoretically tenable. But even in a partial and tentative examination of agricultural protection—taking industrial protection and what other countries do for granted and as inevitable—the student of this problem will be confronted with formidable difficulties. He cannot hope to find a quantitative measurement; at best he will be able to make a qualitative statement of the kind to which Professor Robinson or Professor Nash wisely confined themselves: Our real income would not have been higher if, through less agricultural support, we had devoted fewer resources to agricultural import-saving,* or, in present circumstances, farm output is above the optimum and there would be some economic advantage to the country in releasing from agricultural use some of the resources absorbed by farming in recent years.†

I do not, of course, deny that there might be more

---

* Cf. Austin Robinson, *op. cit.*

† Cf. E. F. Nash, "The Sources of Our Food Supplies," in *Agriculture in the British Economy* (London: Oxford University Press, 1957).

modest, and therefore more realistic, goals for partial and tentative and thus more feasible determinations of the "amounts of protection," especially in the context with which the idea of "bindings" in GATT is concerned. It is precisely for this reason—and, as I said, because it is the *results* of protection that matter and need to be "bound"— that I have proposed a different approach to applying the principle of "no further increase in protection" and verifying compliance."

III. THE PROPOSALS OF THE
INTERNATIONAL CHAMBER OF
COMMERCE

In September, 1963, the International Chamber of Commerce (ICC) released its *Statement on the Expansion of International Trade*. The following paragraphs of the important Recommendations of ICC are concerned with agricultural trade:

Tropical Products

"The ICC generally endorses the resolutions adopted by the Ministerial Meeting of the GATT in May, 1963, relating to the expansion of trade of developing countries. It agrees that tariffs and internal taxes applied to tropical products which do not compete with domestic products should be removed as speedily as possible. In order to take care of the interests of producers who are largely dependent on certain markets where they enjoy preferential treatment, arrangements should be made to help such producers as will initially be adversely affected by the elimination or reduction of present preferences. On the other hand, it would be desirable for all countries exporting tropical products to look to the cheapest markets for their supplies of all kinds.

"Free access to the main markets should be guaranteed, not only for tropical products in their crude form; it should be gradually extended to products having undergone a simple form of processing.

Agricultural Products

"As far as possible the rules recommended for manufactured goods should apply to agricultural products. It is recognized, however, that in many instances the application of such rules would be ineffective or would conflict with the national agricultural policies that exist in practically all countries for a number of deep-seated economic, social, and other reasons, which may be modified but which are unlikely to be abandoned rapidly. The ICC considers that the governments themselves should agree, in those cases, on special rules of negotiation, which may involve the acceptance of a new set of international commitments affecting both exporting and importing countries, including provisions designed to ensure that exporting countries enjoy acceptable terms of access for their products on the markets of other trading nations.

"Various techniques are possible and the ICC intends to submit more specific suggestions as a result of the work of its Commission on Primary Products and Raw Materials. Governments might for instance consider the possibility of negotiating world-wide agreements on a different basis from that of traditional commodity agreements to ensure a better equilibrium between supply and demand and to maintain prices, both on the domestic and world markets, at levels which should be remunerative for reasonably efficient producers and should not artificially encourage uneconomic production. These agreements should take due account of the interests of developing countries that are producers of the commodities in question; they might be supplemented by international arrangements for the disposal of surpluses in the most economically constructive and socially profitable manner. One method would be to see how surpluses should be used in conjunction with schemes for assisting growth in the developing countries through an extension of the present pilot World Food Program. Finally, governments might agree to harmonize their agricultural policies in the context of periodical confrontation exercises organized on a worldwide basis.

"The ICC is convinced that there is a clear interdependence in the proposed trade negotiations between the agricultural and the industrial sectors and that the new trade negotiations will be really successful only if exporters of temperate zone agricultural products or of products competing with the products of that zone derive benefits from the negotiations comparable to those which are expected in the industrial sector."